A Pocketful of
PROMISES

HONOR **HB** BOOKS

Inspiration and Motivation for the Seasons of Life

COOK COMMUNICATIONS MINISTRIES
Colorado Springs, Colorado • Paris, Ontario
KINGSWAY COMMUNICATIONS LTD
Eastbourne, England

Honor Books® is an imprint of
Cook Communications Ministries, Colorado Springs, Colorado 80918
Cook Communications, Paris, Ontario
Kingsway Communications, Eastbourne, England

A Pocketful of Promises
© 2004 by Bordon Books

Printed in Canada
Printing/Year
9 8 7 6 5 / 05 06 07 08

Developed by Bordon Books
6532 E. 71 Street, Suite 105
Tulsa, OK 74133

Unless otherwise noted, Scripture quotations are taken from the King James
Version of the Bible. Scripture quotations marked NASB are taken from the NEW
AMERICAN STANDARD BIBLE®, Copyright © 1960, 1962, 1963, 1968,
1971, 1972, 1973, 1975, 1977, 1995 by The Lockman Foundation. Used by per-
mission; ASV are taken from the American Standard Version © Copyright 1901.
Public Domain; CEV are taken from the Contemporary English Version © 1995 by
American Bible Society. Used by permission; NIV is taken from the HOLY BIBLE,
NEW INTERNATIONAL VERSION®. Copyright © 1973, 1978, 1984
International Bible Society. Used by permission of Zondervan. All rights reserved;
TLB are taken from The Living Bible, © 1971, Tyndale House Publishers, Wheaton,
IL 60189. Used by permission; AMP are taken from the Amplified® Bible,
Copyright © 1954, 1958, 1962, 1964, 1965, 1987 by The Lockman Foundation.
Used by permission; NKJV are taken from the New King James Version®.
Copyright © 1982 by Thomas Nelson, Inc. Used by permission. All rights reserved;
RSV are taken from the Revised Standard Version of the Bible, copyrighted © 1946,
1952, and 1971 by the Division of Christian Education of the Churches of Christ
in the United States of America, and are used by permission. All rights reserved;
NRSV are taken from the New Revised Standard Version of the Bible, copyrighted
by the Division of Christian Education of the National Council of the Churches of
Christ in the United States of America, and are used by permission. NLT are taken
from the New Living Translation copyright © 1996 by Tyndale Charitable Trust.
Used by permission of Tyndale House Publishers; marked NCV are taken from the
New Century Version®. NCV™ Copyright © 1987, 1988, 1991 by Thomas
Nelson, Inc. Used by permission. All rights reserved; NET are from the Holy Bible:
The Net Bible® (New English Translation®). Copyright © 1996, 1997, 1998 by
Biblical Studies Press, LLC. All rights reserved. MSG are taken from The Message.
Copyright © 1993, 1994, 1995, 1996, 2000, 2001, 2002. Used by permission of
NavPress Publishing Group. Used by permission.

ISBN: 1-56292-166-5

Contents

Introduction

Perhaps you've experienced the joy of friendship with someone who knows you, understands you, and loves you when you're not at your best. Most likely, you found that friend offered unconditional love and understanding no matter what circumstance or situation you found yourself in. Imagine your excitement in sharing your life and joy with them. God wants to be that friend to you. You don't have to pick up the telephone or drive across town to be with Him. He is as close as the mention of His name.

God is that encouraging friend, comforter, and the one who can understand you, even when you can't. He wants to be your personal God and confidant. He has given you promises for your life, and He keeps His promises forever. Discover God's voice through His letters to you in *A Pocketful of Promises.*

When we take hold of God's promises, we have all we need to find health and happiness, confidence and contentment, both for this life and the life to come. *A Pocketful of Promises* includes a letter from God to you for daily living that you can apply to your own life. You will also find scriptures and encouraging quotes to help you trust God with even the most important areas of your life. Allow Him to fill you with hope, courage, understanding, and strength through this book.

How to Use *A Pocketful of Promises* in Your Quiet Time

A Pocketful of Promises is more than a book of scriptures arranged by topic. Within the pages you will find an encouraging letter from God regarding each topic, scriptures that offer hope and inspire you to face life's challenges, and a quote to motivate you to rise above the conflict in your heart and mind.

You can use this book in a variety of ways. The following are some suggestions to help you begin to use *A Pocketful of Promises* in your quiet time.

1. Locate the topic you are facing today. They are listed in the table of contents, which we have conveniently placed at the front of the book.

2. Read the section about the topic you are interested in. Break the verses into sections, then ponder and mull over what they mean and are saying to you about God, His character, your life, and your faith.

3. Choose one specific verse to meditate on.

4. Put that verse into your memory, and think about it throughout the day.

5. Personalize the scripture by adding personal pronouns—me, my, I, etc—in place of you, we, and they. Remember, you are in a personal relationship with the God who loves you, so expect Him to speak directly and personally to you.

6. Consider writing in a notebook the things which God has shown you about His promises to you. How do they change your thoughts, feelings, and motivation concerning your situation or circumstances?

Discover what God has to say to you about your life. He cares for you and wants you to know it. Allow Him to fill you with hope, courage, understanding, and strength as your read this book. Have a daily quiet time when you and God can spend regular quality time together. You will find it a practice that will greatly benefit your life.

GOD'S
PROMISES
FOR MY . . .

DOUBTS

My Child,

I know you are struggling with doubt,
but deep inside your spirit I have given
you faith to move mountains. Let My
precious promises wash your doubts away.
I will never leave you, fail you, or forsake
you. I am always with you; you are never
alone. When you feel like giving up, cast
your care and burdens upon Me. Rest in
My arms and trust Me to take care of all
that concerns you. I love you. Lift your
eyes to the Heavens, for I am your help.
Call on Me, and I will restore you. Hope
in Me, for I am here.

~God

God has said, "I will never,
never fail you nor forsake you."
HEBREWS 13:5 TLB

Jesus answered . . . "Truly I say to you,
whoever says to this mountain, 'Be taken
up and cast into the sea,' and does not doubt
in his heart, but believes that what he says
is going to happen, it will be granted him."
MARK 11:22-23 NASB

"Yes, be bold and strong! Banish fear and doubt!
For remember, the Lord your God is with you
wherever you go."
JOSHUA 1:9 TLB

Let us hold firmly to the hope that we have confessed,
because we can trust God to do what he promised.
HEBREWS 10:23 NCV

Jesus answered and said to them, "Truly I say
to you, if you have faith and do not doubt,
you will not only do what was done to the
fig tree, but even if you say to this mountain,
'Be taken up and cast into the sea,' it shall happen."
MATTHEW 21:21 NASB

"When the Son of Man returns, you will know
it beyond all doubt. It will be as evident as
the lightning that flashes across the sky."
LUKE 17:24 NLT

"*I am with you always,
even to the end of the age.*"
(Matthew 28:20 NASB)

DREAMS

Beloved,

Dream big dreams. Many of your dreams are My dreams for your life. I share your excitement for the future, and I have big plans for you. I have held them in My heart since before you were born. I want to see them become a reality as much as you do. Trust Me to fulfill my plans for your life. I have a path in mind for you to follow. Trust and follow Me on your journey. With Me, all things are possible—only believe!

~God

"For I know the plans that I have for you,"
declares the LORD, "plans for welfare and not
for calamity to give you a future and a hope."

JEREMIAH 29:11 NASB

He who began a good work in you will carry it on
to completion until the day of Christ Jesus.

PHILIPPIANS 1:6 NIV

When dreams come true at last,
there is life and joy.

PROVERBS 13:12 TLB

Delight yourself in the LORD; and He will
give you the desires of your heart.

PSALM 37:4 NASB

"In the last days it will be," God declares,
"that I will pour out my Spirit upon all flesh,
and your sons and your daughters shall
prophesy, and your young men shall see visions,
and your old men shall dream dreams."

ACTS 2:17 NRSV

Depend on the Lord in whatever you do,
and your plans will succeed.

PROVERBS 16:3 NCV

*Don't ask yourself what the world needs;
ask yourself what makes you come
alive. And then go and do that.
Because what the world needs is
people who have come alive.*

Dear One,

I am your Father—you belong to Me. I love you with an everlasting love. You are created in My image, and you favor Me. I have filled you with My wisdom and direction. Even as you wouldn't let someone you love fall, I won't let you fall. I want you to come close to Me. Talk to Me and tell Me your heart. I am listening. With patience I wait for you to include Me. You are family, a part of My heart.

~God

We who have been made holy by Jesus,
now have the same Father he has. That is why
Jesus is not ashamed to call us his brothers.

HEBREWS 2:11 TLB

"I will not leave you as orphans; I will come to you."

JOHN 14:18 NASB

See how very much our heavenly Father
loves us, for he allows us to be called
his children, and we really are!

1 JOHN 3:1 NLT

Even if I am delayed, you will know how to live in
the family of God. That family is the church of the
living God, the support and foundation of the truth.

1 TIMOTHY 3:15 NCV

"I will be your father, and you will be my sons
and daughters, says the Lord Almighty."

2 CORINTHIANS 6:18 NCV

For this reason I bow my knees to the Father of
our Lord Jesus Christ, from whom the whole
family in heaven and earth is named.

EPHESIANS 3:14–15 NKJV

Family is God's idea.

FINANCES

Child of Mine,

I am the supplier of your needs.
Although I know what you need before
you ask, I still like to have you to
come to Me and ask, for I am your
provider. Just as an earthly father
desires to give good gifts to his
children, so I desire to give good gifts
to you. I will open the windows of
heaven and pour out a blessing for you.
I have made a provision for your life,
and I desire to see you become a
blessing to others, also.

~God

"Therefore I say to you, do not worry about your life. . . .
Look at the birds of the air, for they neither sow nor
reap nor gather into barns; yet your heavenly Father
feeds them. Are you not of more value than they?"

MATTHEW 6:25–26 NKJV

It is he who will supply all your needs
from his riches in glory, because of
what Christ Jesus has done for us.

PHILIPPIANS 4:19 TLB

He who gathers by labor will increase.

PROVERBS 13:11 NKJV

"Bring all the tithes into the storehouse so there
will be enough food in my Temple. If you do,"
says the LORD Almighty, "I will open the windows
of heaven for you. I will pour out a blessing
so great you won't have enough room to
take it in! Try it! Let me prove it to you!"

MALACHI 3:10 NLT

God *is* able to make all grace abound toward you,
that you, always having all sufficiency in all *things*,
may have an abundance for every good work.

2 CORINTHIANS 9:8 NKJV

"He will give you all you need from day
to day if you live for him and make the
Kingdom of God your primary concern."

MATTHEW 6:33 NLT

*He who is plenteously
provided for from within
needs but little from without.*

FUTURE

Dear Child of God,

I have wonderfully planned your future, and I have filled your life with potential and purpose. My prayer is that you would look to your future with as much pleasure and expectation as I do. My plans are for you to succeed and bring into existence all you were destined for. Hope with earnest expectation for all I have for you. Your future is in My hands, and it can happen as I have dreamed. I love you.

~God

It's in Christ that we find out who we are and
what we are living for. Long before we first
heard of Christ and got our hopes up, he had his
eye on us, had designs on us for glorious living.

EPHESIANS 1:11 THE MESSAGE

I know the plans I have for you, says the Lord.
They are plans for good and not for evil,
to give you a future and a hope.

JEREMIAH 29:11 TLB

"At the time I have decided, my words will come true.
You can trust what I say about the future. It may take
a long time, but keep on waiting—it will happen!"

HABAKKUK 2:3 CEV

Mark the blameless *man,* and observe the upright;
for the future of *that* man *is* peace.

PSALM 37:37 NKJV

Surely goodness and lovingkindness will
follow me all the days of my life, and I will
dwell in the house of the LORD forever.

PSALM 23:6 NASB

The Lord will certainly deliver *and* draw me to
Himself from every assault of evil. He will preserve
and bring [me] safe unto His heavenly kingdom.

2 TIMOTHY 4:18 AMP

I*'ve read the last page
of the Bible, it's all
going to turn out alright.*

LIFE

My Child,

I have given you the choice of life or death. However, I desire for you to choose My ways—eternal life through Christ Jesus. When you choose Me and follow My commandments, you will find yourself eternally nestled in My hand. As long as you choose to follow Me, I will fill you with My joy and give you a long life. Your life is a joy to Me, and you bring Me great pleasure when you stay close to Me. You will receive favor when you seek Me and stay on the path I've set before you. Choose Me.

~God

Choose to love the LORD your God and to obey him
and commit yourself to him, for he is your life.
Then you will live long in the land the LORD swore
to give your ancestors Abraham, Isaac, and Jacob."

DEUTERONOMY 30:20 NLT

You will teach me how to live a holy life.
Being with you will fill me with joy; at
your right hand I will find pleasure forever.

PSALM 16:11 NCV

My child, listen and accept what I say.
Then you will have a long life.

PROVERBS 4:10 NCV

"I give eternal life to them, and they will never perish;
and no one will snatch them out of My hand."

JOHN 10:28 NASB

If the Spirit of Him Who raised up Jesus from
the dead dwells in you, [then] He Who raised
up Christ *Jesus* from the dead will also restore
to life your mortal (short-lived, perishable)
bodies through His Spirit Who dwells in you.

ROMANS 8:11 AMP

Whoever finds me finds life and
receives favor from the LORD.

PROVERBS 8:35 NIV

*L*ife is God's novel. Let him write it.

MARRIAGE

Beloved,

If you and your spouse will build your marriage on the foundation of My love, it will grow stronger each day. Remain patient, kind, and giving toward each other. Live your marriage with honor, and esteem it as precious and worthy of great price. As you allow love to rule in your marriage, you please Me. When you agree, your prayers go unhindered. Ask that I may give you a marriage that honors Me.

~God

Let marriage be held in honor—esteemed worthy, precious [that is], of great price, and especially dear—in all things.

HEBREWS 13:4 AMP

Have unity of spirit, sympathy, love for one another, a tender heart, and a humble mind. Do not repay evil for evil or abuse for abuse; but, on the contrary, repay with a blessing. It is for this that you were called—that you might inherit a blessing.

1 PETER 3:8-9 NRSV

Love has been perfected among us in this: that we may have boldness in the day of judgement; because as He is, so are we in this world. There is no fear in love; but perfect love casts out fear.

1 JOHN 4:17-18 NKJV

He *who* finds a wife finds a *good* thing, and obtains favor from the LORD.

PROVERBS 18:22 NKJV

As the Scriptures say, "A man leaves his father and mother to get married, and he becomes like one person with his wife."

EPHESIANS 5:31 CEV

Husbands, in the same way be considerate as you live with your wives, and treat them with respect as the weaker partner and as heirs with you of the gracious gift of life, so that nothing will hinder your prayers.

1 PETER 3:7 NIV

You will reciprocally promise love, loyalty, and matrimonial honesty. We only want for you this day that these words constitute the principle of your entire life and that with the help of divine grace you will observe these solemn vows that today, before God, you formulate.

 # MISTAKES

Child of Mine,

If you stumble and fall, I will help you up. Humble yourself before Me – for I am rich in mercy toward you. When you make a mistake and fall into sin, be quick to tell Me about it so I can forgive you; and we can go forward as though it never existed. I don't remember your failures, only your successes.

~God

If my people, who are called by my name,
are sorry for what they have done, if they
pray and obey me and stop their evil ways,
I will hear them from heaven. I will forgive
their sin, and I will heal their land.

2 CHRONICLES 7:14 NCV

Depart from evil, and do good;
and dwell for evermore.

PSALM 37:27 ASV

If we confess our sins, he is faithful and
just and will forgive us our sins and
purify us from all unrighteousness.

1 JOHN 1:9 NIV

My little children, I am telling you this so that
you will stay away from sin. But if you sin, there
is someone to plead for you before the Father.
His name is Jesus Christ, the one who is all
that is good and who pleases God completely.

1 JOHN 2:1 TLB

People cannot see their own mistakes.
Forgive me for my secret sins.

PSALM 19:12 NCV

"Those who err in mind will know the truth."

ISAIAH 29:24 NASB

*The greatest mistake we make
is living in constant fear
that we will make one.*

PAST

Dear One,

Look forward instead of backward. Your future is ahead of you, and the past is behind you. I am the creator of new things. When you came to Me, former things passed away and all things were created new. You are growing and becoming new through your relationship with Me. Let go of the past, and press forward to your new adventure in faith.

~God

"Forget the former things; do not dwell on the past.
See, I am doing a new thing! Now it springs up;
do you not perceive it? I am making a way
in the desert and streams in the wasteland."

ISAIAH 43:18-19 NIV

"Behold, I create new heavens and a
new earth; and the former things shall
not be remembered or come into mind."

ISAIAH 65:17 RSV

Behold, *it was* for *my* peace *that* I had great
bitterness: But thou hast in love to my soul
delivered it from the pit of corruption; For
thou hast cast all my sins behind thy back.

ISAIAH 38:17 ASV

He will wipe away every tear from their eyes, and
death will not exist any more—or mourning, or crying,
or pain; the former things have ceased to exist.

REVELATION 21:4 NET

Dear brothers, I am still not all I should be
but I am bringing all my energies to bear
on this one thing: Forgetting the past
and looking forward to what lies ahead.

PHILIPPIANS 3:13 TLB

Those who become Christians become
new persons. They are not the same anymore,
for the old life is gone. A new life has begun!

2 CORINTHIANS 5:17 NLT

I *see not a step before me as I tread on another
year; But I've left the Past in God's keeping—the
Future, His mercy shall clear; And what looks dark
in the distance may brighten as I draw near.*

PROVISION

Dear Child of God,

I have promised to withhold no good thing from you, for you have favor and grace in my sight. I see the big picture of your life and will take good care of you always. Through the twists and turns of life, I will be with you and give you my provision. Remember that I can make a way when there seems to be no way. Look up and hold your head high because you are My child, and I shall supply all your needs.

~Father God

The LORD is my shepherd, I shall not want.

PSALM 23:1 RSV

Your Father knoweth what things
ye have need of, before ye ask him.

MATTHEW 6:8 KJV

His divine power hath given unto us all
things that *pertain* unto life and godliness.

2 PETER 1:3 KJV

My God shall supply all your need according
to his riches in glory by Christ Jesus.

PHILIPPIANS 4:19 KJV

Those who look to the LORD will
have every good thing.

PSALM 34:10 NCV

The LORD will give grace and glory: no good *thing*
will he withhold from them that walk uprightly.

PSALM 84:11 KJV

I *believe God knew and does
know of the need of the
world at this moment.*

My Child,

Let Me teach you the next step of faith for My yoke is easy and My burden is light. My gentleness can make you great. My humility can bring peace to your soul, and My Spirit can fill you with life-giving strength. For it is in Me that you will receive the wisdom to know how much to do and the strength to do it. If you will come near to Me, I will lead you to the green pastures and still waters of My presence.

~God

You let me rest in fields of green grass.
You lead me to streams of peaceful water,
and you refresh my life. You are true to your
name, and you lead me along the right paths.

PSALM 23:2-3 CEV

Come to me, all who labor and are heavy laden,
and I will give you rest.

MATTHEW 11:28 RSV

He said, My presence shall go *with thee*,
and I will give thee rest.

EXODUS 33:14 ASV

There remains therefore a rest
for the people of God.

HEBREWS 4:9 NKJV

"Accept my teachings and learn from me,
because I am gentle and humble in spirit,
and you will find rest for your lives."

MATTHEW 11:29 NCV

My people will live in a peaceful habitation, and in
secure dwellings and in undisturbed resting places.

ISAIAH 32:18 NASB

*People who cannot find time for
recreation are obliged sooner or
later to find time for illness.*

GOD'S PROMISES WHEN I NEED . . .

 ASSURANCE

Beloved,

You may feel powerless, small, and lost in the big picture of your life, but I am your place of safety. I have overcome the world, and My overcoming spirit is in you. Depend on Me, and I will fill your heart with assurance and peace. Just as a small child puts his hand into the hand of his father to cross the street, put your hand in Mine; I will lead you to a safe haven. I loved you enough to die for you; therefore, you can be victorious in this life and forever. Call on Me and I will answer. I am closer than your very breath.

~God

"I am the LORD, your God, who takes
hold of your right hand and says to you,
Do not fear; I will help you."

ISAIAH 41:13 NIV

Give your worries to the LORD, and he will take
care of you. He will never let good people down.

PSALM 55:22 NCV

Overwhelming victory is ours through Christ
who loved us enough to die for us.

ROMANS 8:37 TLB

As far as the east is from the west,
So far has He removed our transgressions from us.

PSALM 103:12 NKJV

"Truly, truly, I say to you, he who hears
My word, and believes Him who sent Me, has
eternal life, and does not come into judgment,
but has passed out of death into life."

JOHN 5:24 NASB

Let us draw near to God with a sincere
heart in full assurance of faith.

HEBREWS 10:22 NIV

*I place no hope in my strength,
nor in my works: but all my
confidence is in God my
protector, who never abandons
those who have put all their
hope and thought in him.*

37

Dear One,

Do not be troubled, but trust in Me. I
will open My everlasting arms and
hold you up in the midst of the sea of
life. Allow My presence to calm your
fears. As a mother comforts her child,
so I will comfort you. I will not send
you away from Me but will draw you
close to My heart. Bask in the fullness
of how much I love you. No matter
what you face in life, remember that I
am standing beside you, lifting you up
and comforting you with My peace. My
grace is sufficient.

~God

The LORD is good, a refuge in times of trouble.
He cares for those who trust in him.

NAHUM 1:7 NIV

Though I am surrounded by troubles,
you will bring me safely through them.
You will clench your fist against my
angry enemies! Your power will save me.

PSALM 138:7 TLB

Even when walking through the dark valley of
death I will not be afraid, for you are close
beside me, guarding, guiding all the way.

PSALM 23:4 TLB

Blessed are those who mourn,
for they will be comforted.

MATTHEW 5:4 NIV

I will not leave you comfortless: I will come to you.

JOHN 14:18 KJV

Praise be to the God and Father of our Lord Jesus
Christ, the Father of compassion and the God of
all comfort, who comforts us in all our troubles, so
that we can comfort those in any trouble with
the comfort we ourselves have received from God.

2 CORINTHIANS 1:3-4 NIV

*God does not comfort us
to make us comfortable,
but to make us comforters.*

COMPASSION

Child of Mine,

Cheer up your soul for I do not want
you to be disgraced, nor do I want your
enemies to rejoice in your defeats. I
know the path you should take and am
ready to point you in the right
direction, no matter how many times
you stumble or go astray. Allow My
truth to lead you. Remember My
unfailing love and compassion, which I
have shown you before. I don't see you
through your failures; I see you through
the eyes of mercy and love. My heart is
full of compassion towards you. Please
receive and accept My love.

~God

The LORD your God is gracious and compassionate, and will not turn *His* face away from you if you return to Him.

2 CHRONICLES 30:9 NASB

Through the LORD's mercies we are not consumed, because His compassions fail not.

LAMENTATIONS 3:22 NKJV

Once again you will have compassion on us. You will trample our sins under your feet and throw them into the depths of the ocean!

MICAH 7:19 NLT

He has made His wonderful works to be remembered; the Lord is gracious, merciful, *and* full of loving compassion.

PSALM 111:4 AMP

The LORD is good to everyone. He showers compassion on all his creation.

PSALM 145:9 NLT

The Lord is full of compassion and mercy.

JAMES 5:11 NIV

I*f I can stop one heart from breaking,*
I shall not live in vain;
If I can ease one life the aching,
Or cool one pain,
Or help one fainting robin
Unto his nest again,
I shall not live in vain.

CONFIDENCE

Dear Child of God,

Be strong and courageous. Do not be afraid, because I go with you. I have given you confidence to do all things through Christ. I helped David slay Goliath and delivered Daniel from the lions' den. Stand and see the salvation of the Lord. Build your confidence in Me. If your hope and mind are stayed on Me, I will give you the courage to overcome the lions and slay the giants in your life. You can do it for I am with you!

~God

Being confident of this very thing, that he
which hath begun a good work in you will
perform *it* until the day of Jesus Christ.

PHILIPPIANS 1:6 KJV

Such confidence as this is ours through Christ
before God. Not that we are competent in
ourselves to claim anything for ourselves,
but our competence comes from God.

2 CORINTHIANS 3:4–5 NIV

The Lord shall be your confidence, firm
and strong, and shall keep your foot from
being caught [in a trap or some hidden danger].

PROVERBS 3:26 AMP

Christ Jesus our Lord, in Whom, because of our
faith in Him, we dare to have the boldness; (courage
and confidence) of free access—an unreserved
approach to God with freedom and without fear.

EPHESIANS 3:11–12 AMP

The LORD himself will go before you. He will be
with you; he will not leave you or forget you.
Don't be afraid and don't worry.

DEUTERONOMY 31:8 NCV

"You can get anything—*anything* you
ask for in prayer—if you believe."

MATTHEW 21:22 TLB

A *perfect faith would lift us
absolutely above fear.*

CONTENTMENT

My Child,

I want you to be content in Me. I am your peace and source of true joy. When you struggle, come to Me; and I will still your restless spirit. Allow Me to fill you with the fruit of the spirit. They are gifts I desire to give you that will bring you great contentment— love, joy, peace, faith. I am all you need to live a contented life. When you follow Me, you follow the highest dreams for your life and fulfillment.

~God

Be content with such things as ye have: for he hath said, I will never leave thee, nor forsake thee.
HEBREWS 13:5 KJV

We know that all things work together for good to them that love God, to them who are the called according to *his* purpose.
ROMANS 8:28 KJV

Godliness with contentment is great gain.
1 TIMOTHY 6:6-8 NIV

He who dwells in the shelter of the Most High will rest in the shadow of the Almighty.
PSALM 91:1 NIV

Those who live following their sinful selves think only about things that their sinful selves want. But those who live following the Spirit are thinking about the things the Spirit wants them to do.
ROMANS 8:5 NCV

All the days of the desponding and afflicted are made evil [by anxious thoughts and forebodings], but he who has a glad heart has a continual feast [regardless of circumstances].
PROVERBS 15:15 AMP

At the heart of the cyclone tearing the sky
And flinging the clouds and the towers by,
Is a place of central calm;
So here in the roar of mortal things,
I have a place where my spirit sings,
In the hollow of God's palm.

45

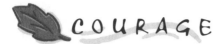 # COURAGE

Beloved,

Take courage because I see the big perspective while your viewpoint of all you are facing is only the size of a keyhole. I know the outcome. When you focus on Me, you will discover a different perspective—a higher perspective. When you are between a rock and a hard place, I will rescue you. Stand still and know that I am God. Ask Me to fill you with a spirit of courage. Be strong and courageous and hope in Me.

~God

Be of good courage, and he shall strengthen
your heart, all ye that hope in the LORD.
PSALM 31:24 KJV

The LORD is my light and my salvation . . . whom
shall I fear? When evil men come to destroy me,
they will stumble and fall! Yes, though a mighty
army marches against me, my heart shall know
no fear! I am confident that God will save me.
PSALM 27:1-3 TLB

I eagerly expect and hope that I will in no way
be ashamed, but will have sufficient courage
so that now as always Christ will be exalted
in my body, whether by life or by death.
PHILIPPIANS 1:20 NIV

But you, be strong and do not lose courage,
for there is reward for your work.
2 CHRONICLES 15:7 NASB

Be strong and of good courage, do not fear or be
in dread of them: for it is the LORD your God who
goes with you; he will not fail you or forsake you.
DEUTERONOMY 31:6 RSV

Christ is faithful as a son over God's house.
And we are his house, if we hold on to our
courage and the hope of which we boast.
HEBREWS 3:6 NIV

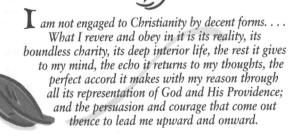

I *am not engaged to Christianity by decent forms. . . .*
What I revere and obey in it is its reality, its
boundless charity, its deep interior life, the rest it gives
to my mind, the echo it returns to my thoughts, the
perfect accord it makes with my reason through
all its representation of God and His Providence;
and the persuasion and courage that come out
thence to lead me upward and onward.

DELIVERANCE

Dear One,

When you cry for help, I will hear you
and deliver you. I am here to rescue
you because you know My name. We
have a relationship of trust and honor.
I will honor you as you honor Me. Your
place is in the light of My glory, which
is removed from all darkness. Hold on
to Me, and I will protect you. As I
delivered the Israelites from the
Egyptians, so will I deliver you from evil
and bring you safely into My kingdom.

~Your Deliverer

Because he cleaves to me in love, I will deliver him;
I will protect him, because he knows my name.
When he calls to me, I will answer him; I will be
with him in trouble, I will rescue him and honor him.
PSALM 91:14–15 RSV

He has rescued us out of the darkness and
gloom of Satan's kingdom and brought us
into the Kingdom of his dear Son.
COLOSSIANS 1:13 TLB

When the righteous cry for help, the LORD hears,
and delivers them out of all their troubles.
PSALM 34:17 RSV

The LORD is my rock, my fortress and my deliverer.
2 SAMUEL 22:2 NIV

He who trusts in his own mind is a fool; but
he who walks in wisdom will be delivered.
PROVERBS 28:26 RSV

The Lord will rescue me from every evil attack
and will bring me safely to his heavenly kingdom.
To him be glory for ever and ever. Amen.
2 TIMOTHY 4:18 NIV

God from the mount of Sinai, whose grey top
Shall tremble, he descending, will himself
In thunder lightning and loud trumpets' sound
Ordain them laws; part such as appertain
To civil justice, part religious rites
Of sacrifice, informing them, by types
And shadows, of that destined
seed to bruise
The serpent, by what means
he shall achieve
Mankind's deliverance.

ENCOURAGEMENT

Child of Mine,

Don't be tempted to give in to discouragement and frustration if the realities of life have thrown your plans into disarray. Look to My Word for encouragement. Take comfort in knowing that I love you and have filled your life with My presence. Submit yourself and your plans to me. Break forth with singing, and shout to the mountaintops with praise. I love you and care for you, so build yourself up through praising Me, and watch your joy return. For as you focus on Me, your discouragement will flee.

~God

Do not gloat over me, my enemy!
Though I have fallen, I will rise. Though I
sit in darkness, the LORD will be my light.

MICAH 7:8 NIV

"Don't lose your courage or be afraid.
Don't panic or be frightened, because the Lord
your God goes with you, to fight for you
against your enemies and to save you."

DEUTERONOMY 20:3-4 NCV

Take delight in the Lord, and he will
give you the desires of your heart.

PSALM 37:4 NRSV

I can do all things in him who strengthens me.

PHILIPPIANS 4:13 RSV

Be strong and do not let your hands be weak,
for your work shall be rewarded!

2 CHRONICLES 15:7 NKJV

If we are faithful to the end, trusting God
just as firmly as when we first believed,
we will share in all that belongs to Christ.

HEBREWS 3:14 NLT

*A good word costs no more
than a bad one.*

ENDURANCE

Dear Child of God,

Don't give up, but stand firm. I have given you the strength to endure hard times and come through victoriously. Your triumphs don't depend on you alone. Lean on Me, and I will help you reach your goal. Your life is in the palm of My hand, and your future is secure with Me. I want to see your dreams realized because I gave many of them to you. Let Me fill you with My Spirit of endurance, for I finished My course, and you will finish yours also.

~Jesus

I have fought the good fight, I have finished the race,
I have kept the faith. Finally, there is laid up for me the
crown of righteousness, which the Lord, the righteous
Judge, will give to me on that Day, and not to me
only but also to all who have loved His appearing.

2 TIMOTHY 4:7–8 NKJV

If you suffer for doing good and you endure it,
this is commendable before God.

1 PETER 2:20 NIV

Brethren, I do not regard myself as having laid
hold of *it* yet; but one thing I *do:* forgetting what
lies behind and reaching forward to what *lies*
ahead, I press on toward the goal for the prize
of the upward call of God in Christ Jesus.

PHILIPPIANS 3:13–14 NASB

After he had patiently endured,
he obtained the promise.

HEBREWS 6:15 KJV

Be strong and steady, always enthusiastic
about the Lord's work, for you know that
nothing you do for the Lord is ever useless.

1 CORINTHIANS 15:58 NLT

My brethern, count it all joy when ye fall
into divers temptations; knowing *this,* that
the trying of your faith worketh patience.
But let patience have *her* perfect work, that
ye may be perfect and entire, wanting nothing.

JAMES 1:2–4 KJV

*Endurance is the crowning quality,
And patience all the passion
of great hearts.*

FAITH

My Child,

Faith is the substance of things hoped for and the evidence of things not seen. I challenge you to believe in Me and trust the wonderful promises I have given you. Nurture your faith with My Word and prayer. Let Me give you the strength and power to fulfill your destiny. Let Me be the anchor for your soul, so you won't drift into the sea of doubt and unbelief.

~God

[Jesus] said to them: . . . "Truly I say to you, if you have faith the size of a mustard seed, you will say to this mountain, 'Move from here to there,' and it will move; and nothing will be impossible to you."

MATTHEW 17:20 NASB

Every child of God can defeat the world, and our faith is what gives us this victory.

1 JOHN 5:4 CEV

"And in that day ye shall ask me nothing. Verily, verily, I say unto you, Whatsoever ye shall ask the Father in my name, he will give *it* you. Hitherto have ye asked nothing in my name: ask, and ye shall receive, that your joy may be full."

JOHN 16:23-24 KJV

Without faith *it is* impossible to please *him:* for he that cometh to God must believe that he is, and *that* he is a rewarder of them that diligently seek him.

HEBREWS 11:6 KJV

"I assure you, most solemnly I tell you, if anyone steadfastly believes in Me, he will himself be able to do the things that I do; and he will do even greater things than these, because I go to the Father."

JOHN 14:12 AMP

God has dealt to each one a measure of faith.

ROMANS 12:3 NKJV

No man can create faith in himself. Something must happen to him which [Martin] Luther calls "the divine work in us," which changes us, gives us new birth, and makes us completely different people in heart, spirit, mind, and all our powers.

FAVOR

Beloved,

You are the apple of My eye. Esteem My favor highly, and know that when you put Me first in everything you do, I will surround you with a shield of favor. I love you and want the very best for you. I desire to bless you at all times and fulfill My wonderful plans for your life. Trust that My power will open doors for you and My hand will be upon your life. The good work I began in you, I will bring to completion.

~God

Surely, O LORD, you bless the righteous; you surround them with your favor as with a shield.

PSALM 5:12 NIV

They did not conquer by their own strength and skill, but by your mighty power and because you smiled upon them and favored them.

PSALM 44:3 TLB

May the favor of the Lord our God rest upon us; establish the work of our hands for us— yes, establish the work of our hands.

PSALM 90:17 NIV

In everything you do, put God first, and he will direct you and crown your efforts with success.

PROVERBS 3:6 TLB

"Whoever finds me finds life and receives favor from the LORD."

PROVERBS 8:35 NIV

A *good* name is to be more desired than great wealth, favor is better than silver and gold.

PROVERBS 22:1 NASB

It is most appropriate that a people whose storehouses have been so lavishly filled with all the fruits of the earth by the gracious favor of God should manifest their gratitude by large gifts to His suffering children in other lands.

GRACE

Dear One,

I am your Light and your Salvation. I
long to pour out My grace and glory
upon you. I will honor your love and
commitment to Me. For you are My
treasure and are so precious to Me. My
grace and mercy will follow you all the
days of your life. Let Me transform you
into the person you long to become.

~God

Sin will have no dominion over you, since you
are not under law but under grace. What then?
Should we sin because we are not under
law but under grace? By no means!

ROMANS 6:14–15 NRSV

You know the grace of our Lord Jesus Christ, that
although he was rich, he became poor for your
sakes, so that you by his poverty could become rich.

2 CORINTHIANS 8:9 NET

"My grace is all you need, for my
power is perfected in weakness."

2 CORINTHIANS 12:9 ISV

We believe that through the grace
of the Lord Jesus Christ we shall be
saved in the same manner as they.

ACTS 15:11 NKJV

God is able to make all grace overflow to
you so that because you have enough of
everything in every way at all times,
you will overflow in every good work.

2 CORINTHIANS 9:8 NET

Where sin increased, grace increased all the more.

ROMANS 5:20 NIV

*Grace is God himself, his loving
energy at work within his
church and within our souls.*

GUIDANCE

Child of Mine,

You have a choice —to lean on your own understanding or to trust Me. I am calling you to walk by faith and not by sight. I have ordered your steps in the way you should go, and I will teach you My ways as I walk with you one step at a time. I will provide the answers you need and show you which way to turn. I am your Guide and Helper. Do not choose to go your own way, for that is the path of destruction. I will lead you on the path of eternal life. Follow Me.

~God

This God is our God for ever and ever;
he will be our guide even to the end.

PSALM 48:14 NIV

The mind of man plans his way, but
the LORD directs his steps.

PROVERBS 16:9 NASB

The steps of a *good* man are ordered by the LORD:
and he delighteth in his way.

PSALM 37:23 KJV

I will instruct you (says the Lord) and guide you
along the best pathway for your life; I will
advise you and watch your progress.

PSALM 32:8 TLB

Trust in the LORD with all thine heart; and lean not
unto thine own understanding. In all thy ways
acknowledge him, and he shall direct thy paths.

PROVERBS 3:5-6 KJV

Thy word *is* a lamp unto my feet,
and a light unto my path.

PSALM 119:105 KJV

*H*ere I pause in my sojourning,
giving thanks for having come,
come to trust, at every turning,
God will guide me safely home.

HAPPINESS

Dear Child of God,

Everlasting happiness comes from your
relationship with Me. As you spend
time with Me, your heart will be
gladdened and you will be happy from
the inside out. I will fill your day with
small pleasures that bring you joy.
Pause, and look at the little gifts I give
you to bring a smile to your heart.
Allow My goodness and My presence to
bring laughter and fulfillment to your
daily life.

~God

A glad heart makes a cheerful countenance.

PROVERBS 15:13 AMP

To the man who pleases him God gives
wisdom and knowledge and joy.

ECCLESIASTES 2:26 RSV

You will teach me how to live a holy life.
Being with you will fill me with joy; at
your right hand I will find pleasure forever.

PSALM 16:11 NCV

The one whom God corrects is happy, so do
not hate being corrected by the Almighty.

JOB 5:17 NCV

Happy are the people whose God is the LORD.

PSALM 144:15 NRSV

Happy are those who are helped by the God
of Jacob. Their hope is in the LORD their God.

PSALM 146:5 NCV

*Happiness does not notice
the passing of time.*

HEALTH & HEALING

My Child,

My desire is for you to live in health all the days of your life. Bring Me your pain, sorrow, and grief; and I will give you joy and health. Hold on to Me because I am your strength. I want you to live out all the days of your life and fulfill every plan I have set before you. I am the Lord Who heals you.

~God

Yes, I will bless the Lord and not forget
the glorious things he does for me.
He forgives all my sins. He heals me.
PSALM 103:2-3 TLB

If you do these things, your salvation will come
like the dawn. Yes, your healing will come quickly.
Your godliness will lead you forward, and the
glory of the LORD will protect you from behind.
ISAIAH 58:8 NLT

"I will restore you to health
And I will heal you of your wounds,"
declares the LORD.
JEREMIAH 30:17 NASB

Surely He has borne our griefs And carried our
sorrows; Yet we esteemed Him stricken, Smitten
by God, and afflicted. But He *was* wounded
for our transgressions, He *was* bruised for our
iniquities; the chastisement for our peace *was*
upon Him, And by His stripes we are healed.
ISAIAH 53:4-5 NKJV

"I am the LORD, who heals you."
EXODUS 15:26 NIV

"You who fear my name, the Sun of Righteousness
will rise with healing in his wings. And you will go
free, leaping with joy like calves let out to pasture."
MALACHI 4:2 TLB

Praise to the Lord, the Almighty,
who rules all creation!
O my soul, worship the source
of thy health and salvation!

HOPE

Beloved,

Hope is an earnest expectation—so have an earnest expectation of Me. Believe I love you and want the very best for you. Be encouraged in My Word, and know that I desire to see you achieve great things in your life. Experience joy in My presence, and encourage your heart by knowing that I desire to see you accomplish your purpose. Hang your hope on Me, and trust that I will fulfill My plans for you.

~God

I pray also that the eyes of your heart may be enlightened in order that you may know the hope to which he has called you, the riches of his glorious inheritance in the saints, and his incomparably great power for us who believe.

EPHESIANS 1:18–19 NIV

Be of good courage, and he shall strengthen your heart, all ye that hope in the LORD.

PSALM 31:24 KJV

Praise God, the Father of our Lord Jesus Christ. God is so good, and by raising Jesus from death, he has given us new life and a hope that lives on.

1 PETER 1:3 CEV

May the God of hope fill you with all joy and peace in believing, that you may abound in hope by the power of the Holy Spirit.

ROMANS 15:13 NASB

O Lord, you alone are my hope; I've trusted you from childhood.

PSALM 71:5 TLB

Everything that was written in the past was written to teach us, so that through endurance and the encouragement of the Scriptures we might have hope.

ROMANS 15:4 NIV

Our God, our help in ages past,
Our hope for years to come. . . .

JOY

Dear One,

Your joy is never dependent on outward circumstances, but rather on an inward gift that comes from Me. I can wipe away your tears and take away the pain. Let Me pour My joy out on you. Come to Me, and let Me fill you with My presence. Allow My joy to bubble up within you like a fresh spring renewing your heart and showing you the path to eternal life.

~God

May those who sow in tears reap with shouts
of joy! He that goes forth weeping, bearing
the seed for sowing, shall come home with
shouts of joy, bringing his sheaves with him.

PSALM 126:5-6 RSV

He will yet fill your mouth with laughter
and your lips with shouts of joy.

JOB 8:21 TLB

The joy of the Lord is your strength.

NEHEMIAH 8:10 KJV

You will show me the path of life;
In Your presence *is* fullness of joy;
At Your right hand *are* pleasures forevermore.

PSALM 16:11 NKJV

Light shines on those who do right;
joy belongs to those who are honest.

PSALM 97:11 NCV

Be joyful always; pray continually; give
thanks in all circumstances, for this is
God's will for you in Christ Jesus.

1 THESSALONIANS 5:16-18 NIV

*Joy is peace dancing and
peace is joy at rest.*

PATIENCE

Child of Mine,

I know you find it difficult at times to remain patient. Look at patience as if you were a farmer waiting for a field to grow. Before he is able to harvest his reward, he must diligently wait for the right season. Allow Me to work out things for good in your life, and give Me time to do it. Cast your anxieties on Me, and rest in My love. You will have your answers in due season, because patience will bring reward to your life.

~God

My brethren, count it all joy when you fall into
various trials, knowing that the testing of your
faith produces patience. But let patience
have *its* perfect work, that you may be
perfect and complete, lacking nothing.

JAMES 1:2-4 NKJV

You need to keep on patiently doing
God's will if you want him to do for
you all that he has promised.

HEBREWS 10:36 TLB

I waited patiently for the LORD to help me,
and he turned to me and heard my cry.

PSALM 40:1 NLT

Be humble and gentle. Be patient with
each other, making allowance for each
other's faults because of your love.

EPHESIANS 4:2 TLB

Be like those who through faith and patience
will receive what God has promised.

HEBREWS 6:12 NCV

Be patient and stand firm,
because the Lord's coming is near.

JAMES 5:8 NIV

*No man can learn patience except by
going out into the hurly-burly world
and taking life just as it blows.
Patience is riding out the gale.*

Dear Child of God,

Great is the peace and undisturbed composure of those who trust in Me. I desire to give you peace like a river that flows on and on. Even when it seems as if you are experiencing a drought in your life, when you feel parched by life's trials, the river of life flows from My throne to your heart. Like the water flowing through the land providing water for life, so My life-giving peace flows to you. You are a tree planted by My rivers of living water. Stay close to the peaceful waters of My Spirit.

~God

Consider the blameless, observe the upright;
there is a future for the man of peace.

PSALM 37:37 NIV

The peace of God, which passeth all
understanding, shall keep your hearts
and minds through Christ Jesus.

PHILIPPIANS 4:7 KJV

He will keep in perfect peace all those who trust in
him, whose thoughts turn often to the Lord!

ISAIAH 26:3 TLB

Since we have been justified through faith, we have
peace with God through our Lord Jesus Christ.

ROMANS 5:1 NIV

"Blessed *are* the peacemakers,
for they shall be called sons of God."

MATTHEW 5:9 NKJV

"I am leaving you with a gift—peace of mind and
heart. And the peace I give isn't like the peace
the world gives. So don't be troubled or afraid."

JOHN 14:27 NLT

*Then pealed the bells more loud and deep:
"God is not dead; nor doth He sleep;
The wrong shall fail,
The right prevail,
With peace on earth,
good will to men."*

PERSEVERANCE

My Child,

Stand fast and hold tightly to Me. I love you and have given you everlasting consolation and good hope through grace. Comfort your heart for I have established you in every good word and work. I hear your prayers and listen to the words that you speak. I will uphold your soul. Hold on to all I have promised, and you will see My faithfulness and fruit in your life.

~God

You need to persevere so that when you
have done the will of God, you will
receive what he has promised.
HEBREWS 10:36 NIV

Blessed is the man who endures trial, for when he
has stood the test he will receive the crown of life,
which God has promised to those who love him.
JAMES 1:12 RSV

We also exult in our tribulations, knowing
that tribulation brings about perseverance;
and perseverance, proven character;
and proven character, hope.
ROMANS 5:3-4 NASB

Consider it pure joy, my brothers, whenever you
face trials of many kinds, because you know that
the testing of your faith develops perseverance.
Perseverance must finish its work so that you may
be mature and complete, not lacking anything.
JAMES 1:2-4 NIV

He will keep you strong to the end, so that you will
be blameless on the day of our Lord Jesus Christ.
1 CORINTHIANS 1:8 NIV

We are hard pressed on every side, but not crushed;
perplexed, but not in despair; persecuted, but not
abandoned; struck down, but not destroyed.
2 CORINTHIANS 4:8-9 NIV

*Nothing great was ever done
without much enduring.*

PROSPERITY

Beloved,

I take pleasure in your prosperity, and I truly enjoy meeting your needs. I desire to bless you with My abundance so that you can be a blessing to others and confirm My covenant with you. I want to give you good gifts—it thrills Me most when you acknowledge Me as your perfect gift and embrace my love. For these are the gifts that endure.

~God

Seek ye first the kingdom of God,
and his righteousness; and all these
things shall be added unto you.
MATTHEW 6:33 KJV

If they obey and serve him, they will spend the rest of
their days in prosperity and their years in contentment.
JOB 36:11 NIV

Every one that hath forsaken houses, or brethren,
or sisters, or father, or mother, or wife, or children,
or lands, for my name's sake, shall receive an
hundredfold, and shall inherit everlasting life.
MATTHEW 19:29 KJV

If you carefully obey the rules and regulations which
he gave to Israel through Moses, you will prosper.
Be strong and courageous, fearless and enthusiastic!
1 CHRONICLES 22:13 TLB

Carefully follow the terms of this covenant,
so that you may prosper in everything you do.
DEUTERONOMY 29:9 NIV

Let them shout for joy and rejoice,
who favor my vindication;
And let them say continually,
"The LORD be magnified,
Who delights in the prosperity of His servant."
PSALM 35:27 NASB

*Everything we are given and everything
we are deprived of is nothing but a finger
pointing out the direction of God's hidden
promise which we shall taste in full.*

PROTECTION

Dear One,

Come and live with Me in the secret place, and I will shadow you with My wings. I am your refuge and fortress: trust Me. I will deliver you. My truth is your shield. You have no reason to fear or become terrified. While a thousand fall at your side, and ten thousand at your right hand, evil won't come near you. Only with your eyes will you see the reward of the wicked because you set your love on Me. I have given My angels charge over you to keep you safe. With long life I satisfy you and show you My salvation.

~God

The Angel of the Lord guards and
rescues all who reverence him.

PSALM 34:7 TLB

Fear not, for I am with you, be not dismayed, for I
am your God; I will strengthen you, I will help you,
I will uphold you with my victorious right hand.

ISAIAH 41:10 RSV

The Lord is faithful, and He will strengthen
and protect you from the evil *one*.

2 THESSALONIANS 3:3 NASB

The Lord is a strong fortress.
The godly run to him and are safe.

PROVERBS 18:10 TLB

The LORD shall preserve you from all evil;
He shall preserve your soul. The LORD shall
preserve your going out and your coming in
From this time forth, and even forevermore.

PSALM 121:7-8 NKJV

He that dwelleth in the secret place of the most
High shall abide under the shadow of the Almighty.
I will say of the LORD, *He is* my refuge and
my fortress: my God; in him will I trust.

PSALM 91:1-2 KJV

*God incarnate is the end of
fear; and the heart that realizes
that he is in the midst . . . will
be quiet in the midst of alarm.*

REDEMPTION

Child of Mine,

I bought you with a precious price and consider you worth the sacrifice. Your salvation is secure through the gift Jesus made in His death, burial, and resurrection. You are pardoned, and your sin is no longer a memory. It is forgotten—washed away in the flow of the blood of Jesus. I love you.

~God

When the fullness of time had come, God sent his
Son, born of a woman, born under the law, in order
to redeem those who were under the law, so that
we might receive adoption as his children.
GALATIANS 4:4-5 ISV

As for those who serve the Lord,
he will redeem them; everyone who
takes refuge in him will be freely pardoned.
PSALM 34:22 TLB

Not with the blood of goats and calves, but with
his own blood he went into the Holy of Holies
once for all and secured our eternal redemption.
HEBREWS 9:12 ISV

All have sinned, and come short of the glory of
God; being justified freely by his grace through
the redemption that is in Christ Jesus.
ROMANS 3:23-24 KJV

He has rescued us from the power of darkness and
transferred us into the kingdom of his beloved Son, in
whom we have redemption, the forgiveness of sins.
COLOSSIANS 1:13-14 NRSV

In him we have redemption through his blood,
the forgiveness of sins, in accordance with the
riches of God's grace that he lavished on us
with all wisdom and understanding.
EPHESIANS 1:7-8 NIV

God is my strong salvation,
What foe have I to fear?
In darkness and temptation,
My light, my help is near.

81

RESTORATION

Dear Child of God,

I am your Restorer. In My lovingkindness
I will restore to you the years that have
been wasted or eaten away by the evil
one. I will strengthen you and raise
you up. I will forgive your sins and
restore to you the joy of My salvation. I
will satisfy you with My presence and
fill you with My Spirit.

~Your Restorer

Turn to God! Give up your sins, and you will be
forgiven. Then that time will come when
the Lord will give you fresh strength.

ACTS 3:19-20 CEV

The God of all grace, who called you to
his eternal glory in Christ, after you have
suffered a little while, will himself restore you
and make you strong, firm and steadfast.

1 PETER 5:10 NIV

He restores my soul.

PSALM 23:3 NKJV

Restore to me again the joy of your salvation,
and make me willing to obey you.

PSALM 51:12 TLB

Though you have made me see troubles, many
and bitter, you will restore my life again; from the
depths of the earth you will again bring me up.

PSALM 71:20 NIV

Be made new in the attitude of your minds;
and . . . put on the new self, created to be
like God in true righteousness and holiness.

EPHESIANS 4:23-24 NIV

*Lord Jesus, You died to help me die.
Take my life. I draw no protective line
around anything that needs to go.*

SELF-CONTROL

My Child,

I have given you the spirit of power so that you can direct your steps in the path of righteousness. Your body is the temple of My Spirit, so lend yourself to the things that please Me. Don't allow your impulses or your emotions to rule your life, but rather give yourself over to Me; and let My Spirit empower you to live a life for Me.

~God

Stop depriving one another, except by agreement
for a time so that you may devote yourselves to
prayer, and come together again lest Satan will
tempt you because of your lack of self-control.
1 CORINTHIANS 7:5 NASB

Above all else, guard your heart,
for it affects everything you do.
PROVERBS 4:23 NLT

Knowing God leads to self-control.
Self-control leads to patient endurance,
and patient endurance leads to godliness.
2 PETER 1:6 NLT

He who guards his mouth and his tongue
keeps himself from troubles.
PROVERBS 21:23 AMP

Every man that striveth for the mastery is
temperate in all things. Now they *do it* to obtain
a corruptible crown; but we an incorruptible.
1 CORINTHIANS 9:25 KJV

Brothers and sisters, you have no obligation
whatsoever to do what your sinful nature urges you
to do. If you keep on following it, you will perish.
But if through the power of the Holy Spirit you
turn from it and its evil deeds, you will live.
ROMANS 8:12-13 NLT

*Self-control is the ability to
keep cool while someone is
making it hot for you.*

Beloved,

In times of trouble and chaos, depend on Me. I will quiet your fears and proclaim peace to the storms in your life. Meditate on My faithfulness, for I will never leave you or forsake you. When you call to Me, I will answer you. No matter how rough the water, I will steady your ship. Keep your eyes on Me, for I will always be with you. I am the anchor of your soul.

~God

Wisdom and knowledge will be
the stability of your times,
And the strength of salvation;
The fear of the LORD *is* His treasure.

ISAIAH 33:6 NKJV

If we are faithful to the end, trusting God just
as we did when we first became Christians,
we will share in all that belongs to Christ.

HEBREWS 3:14 TLB

He will not fear evil tidings; his heart
is steadfast, trusting in the LORD.

PSALM 112:7 NASB

Be steadfast, immovable, always
abounding in the work of the Lord, knowing
that your labor is not in vain in the Lord.

1 CORINTHIANS 15:58 NKJV

He is the living God, and steadfast for ever,
and his kingdom that which shall not be destroyed;
and his dominion shall be even unto the end.

DANIEL 6:26 ASV

Grass withers and flowers fade, but
the word of our God endures forever.

ISAIAH 40:8 TEV

*Stability is found in God's
unfailing love.*

STRENGTH

Dear One,

I created you to need Me. You have
little strength apart from Me. Yet
when you recognize your weakness and
humbly seek my face, I, The Lord
Omnipotent, become your strength.
Then you will find the grace and
strength to proclaim, "The Lord is the
strength of my life." I long to show
myself strong on your behalf. Will you
entrust yourself to Me and let Me
strengthen the knees that are feeble?

~God

He will give his people strength.
He will bless them with peace.

PSALM 29:11 TLB

I can do everything through him
who gives me strength.

PHILIPPIANS 4:13 NIV

He giveth power to the faint; and to *them
that have* no might he increaseth strength.

ISAIAH 40:29 KJV

They that wait upon the Lord shall renew
their strength. They shall mount up with
wings like eagles; they shall run and not
be weary; they shall walk and not faint.

ISAIAH 40:31 TLB

"My grace is sufficient for you, for My
strength is made perfect in weakness."

2 CORINTHIANS 12:9 NKJV

My flesh and my heart fail;
But God *is* the strength of my
heart and my portion forever.

PSALM 73:26 NKJV

*God is waiting eagerly to respond with
new strength to each little act of
self-control, small disciplines of prayer,
feeble searching after him. And his
children shall be filled if they will only
hunger and thirst after what he offers.*

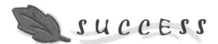 # SUCCESS

Child of Mine,

I have plans for your life that will lead you down the road of true success, but My eternal plans require external perspective. Don't become discouraged when you stumble and fall, for I have called and anointed you. I will accompany you for the entire journey. I desire to see you as the head and not the tail. So stay close to Me, and allow Me to work in your life. Follow My instructions, and you will achieve everlasting success.

~God

The LORD will grant you abundant prosperity—in the fruit of your womb, the young of your livestock and the crops of your ground—in the land he swore to your forefathers to give you. The LORD will open the heavens, the storehouse of his bounty, to send rain on your land in season and to bless all the work of your hands. You will lend to many nations but will borrow from none.

DEUTERONOMY 28:11–12 NIV

True humility and respect for the Lord lead
a man to riches, honor and long life.

PROVERBS 22:4 TLB

This book of the law shall not depart out of your mouth, but you shall meditate on it day and night, that you may be careful to do according to all that is written in it; for then you shall make your way prosperous, and then you shall have good success.

JOSHUA 1:8 RSV

It is not that we think we can do
anything of lasting value by ourselves.
Our only power and success come from God.

2 CORINTHIANS 3:5 NLT

Surely I know the plans I have for you,
says the Lord, plans for your welfare and
not for harm, to give you a future with hope.

JEREMIAH 29:11 NRSV

He had great success in everything
he did because the Lord was with him.

1 SAMUEL 18:14 NCV

*Success is not a place at which
one arrives but rather . . . the
spirit with which one undertakes
and continues the journey.*

UNDERSTANDING

Dear Child of God,

It is hard for you to understand life without My illumination upon your heart and mind. Will you make your ear attentive to My wisdom? Will you incline your heart to My understanding? Ask Me to give you understanding so that you can know Me and walk in My ways. And also that you can be a blessing to those around you. I will surely answer your hearts cry, for I delight in you.

~God

Yes, if you want better insight and discernment, and are searching for them as you would for lost money or hidden treasure, then wisdom will be given you, and knowledge of God himself; you will soon learn the importance of reverence for the Lord and of trusting him. For the Lord grants wisdom! His every word is a treasure of knowledge and understanding.

PROVERBS 2:3-6 TLB

The entrance of Your words gives light;
It gives understanding to the simple.

PSALM 119:130 NKJV

Trust in the LORD with all thine heart; and
lean not unto thine own understanding.

PROVERBS 3:5 KJV

Good understanding produces favor.

PROVERBS 13:15 NASB

Discretion will guard you,
Understanding will watch over you,
To deliver you from the way of evil,
From the man who speaks perverse things.

PROVERBS 2:11-12 NASB

Call to Me and I will answer you, and I will tell you
great and mighty things, which you do not know.

JEREMIAH 33:3 NASB

*The heart has its reasons,
which reason knows not of.*

WISDOM

My Child,

If you lack wisdom, you only need to ask Me and I will give it to you, for I give good gifts to My children. Wisdom is the principle thing, so get wisdom. It is more valuable than money, status, fame, or fortune. So let your heart retain My words, for they contain the seeds of supernatural wisdom that will be planted in your heart.

~God

There shall be stability in your times, an abundance
of salvation, wisdom, and knowledge; the reverent
fear *and* worship of the Lord is your treasure *and* His.
ISAIAH 33:6 AMP

In him we have redemption through his blood,
the forgiveness of sins, in accordance with the
riches of God's grace that he lavished on us
with all wisdom and understanding
EPHESIANS 1:7-8 NIV

If you want to know what God wants you to do,
ask him, and he will gladly tell you, for he is
always ready to give a bountiful supply of wisdom
to all who ask him; he will not resent it.
JAMES 1:5 TLB

If any of you needs wisdom, you should
ask God for it. He is generous and enjoys
giving to all people, so he will give you wisdom.
JAMES 1:5 NCV

To the man who pleases him, God gives wisdom,
knowledge and happiness.
ECCLESIASTES 2:26 NIV

The knowledge of the Holy One is understanding.
For by me your days will be multiplied,
and years of life will be added to you.
PROVERBS 9:10-11 NASB

*God, give us grace to accept with serenity
the things that cannot be changed,
courage to change the things which
should be changed and the wisdom to
distinguish the one from the other.*

GOD'S
PROMISES
WHEN
I FEEL . . .

ANGRY

Beloved,

I am here to heal your emotions. Give
Me your anger, and draw strength from
Me. Just as I offer forgiveness, you can
choose to forgive those who have angered
you. I will make a way for healing and
restoration if you will open the door for
Me in this situation. Follow My lead,
and watch lovingkindness flow from
your heart to the one who has hurt you.
I have a higher perspective, and I will
show you how to forgive if you will ask
Me. Let go, and allow Me to fill you
with My peace. I love you.

~God

He *that is* slow to anger is better than the mighty;
and he that ruleth his spirit than he that taketh a city.
PROVERBS 16:32 KJV

Good sense makes a man slow to anger,
and it is his glory to overlook an offense.
PROVERBS 19:11 RSV

A wise man controls his temper.
He knows that anger causes mistakes.
PROVERBS 14:29 TLB

Those who control their anger have
great understanding; those with
a hasty temper will make mistakes.
PROVERBS 14:29 NLT

Do everything without complaining or arguing. Then
you will be innocent and without any wrong. You
will be God's children without fault. But you are
living with crooked and mean people all around you,
among whom you shine like stars in the dark world.
PHILIPPIANS 2:14-15 NCV

I'm telling you to love your enemies. Let them bring
out the best in you, not the worst. When someone
gives you a hard time, respond with the energies of
prayer, for then you are working out of your true
selves, your God-created selves. This is what God
does. He gives his best—the sun to warm and
the rain to nourish—to everyone, regardless:
the good and bad, the nice and nasty.
MATTHEW 5:44-45 THE MESSAGE

Anger kills both laughter and joy;
what greater foe is there than anger?

ANXIOUS

Dear One,

Pursue Me, and don't fuss about what's on the table at mealtimes or whether the clothes in your closet are in fashion. There is far more to your life than the food you put in your stomach and more to your appearance than the clothes you hang on your body. If I give much attention to the appearance of wildflowers, I will attend to you, take pride in you, and do the best for you. Focus your attention on Me, and trust My provisions in your life. Don't worry about missing out. You'll find that all of your everyday concerns will be taken care of. Give your entire attention to what I'm doing right now, and don't worry about what may or may not happen tomorrow. I'll help you when that time comes. Don't let anxiety and fear rob you of living and enjoying today. It is My gift to you.

~God

Do not be anxious about anything. Instead tell
your requests to God in your every prayer and
petition—with thanksgiving. And the peace of
God that surpasses all understanding will guard
your hearts and minds in Christ Jesus.

PHILIPPIANS 4:6-7 NET

For I, the LORD your God, hold your right hand;
it is I who say to you, "Fear not, I will help you."

ISAIAH 41:13 RSV

These things I have spoken unto you,
that in me ye might have peace. In the
world ye shall have tribulation: but be of
good cheer; I have overcome the world.

JOHN 16:33 KJV

Therefore humble yourselves under the mighty hand
of God, that He may exalt you in due time, casting
all your care upon Him, for He cares for you.

1 PETER 5:6-7 NKJV

Cast thy burden upon the LORD,
and he shall sustain thee.

PSALM 55:22 KJV

Come to me, all you who are weary and
burdened, and I will give you rest.

MATTHEW 11:28 NET

*It ain't no use putting up your
umbrella till it rains.*

CONFUSED

Child of Mine,

I am not the author of confusion. Rather, I am the Shepherd of your soul. I desire to lead you, My sheep, into the green pastures of peace and confidence. When you feel confused, come to Me; and I will settle your mind until you can hear Me clearly again. I can replace uncertainty with wisdom, shine the light of truth on the situations in your life, and set you free to make good choices.

~God

If you want to know what God wants you to do,
ask him, and he will gladly tell you, for he is always
ready to give a bountiful supply of wisdom
to all who ask him; he will not resent it.

JAMES 1:5 TLB

Trust the Lord with all your heart, and don't depend
on your own understanding. Remember the Lord
in all you do, and he will give you success.

PROVERBS 3:5-6 NCV

Instead of your shame *you shall have* double *honor,*
And *instead of* confusion they shall
rejoice in their portion. Therefore in
their land they shall possess double;
Everlasting joy shall be theirs.

ISAIAH 61:7 NKJV

The fear of man bringeth a snare: but whoso
putteth his trust in the LORD shall be safe.

PROVERBS 29:25 KJV

Your ears will hear a word behind you,
"This is the way, walk in it," whenever
you turn to the right or to the left.

ISAIAH 30:21 NASB

The path of the righteous is like the light of dawn,
which shines brighter and brighter until full day.

PROVERBS 4:18 NRSV

T*ruth frees you from confusion.*

103

DISAPPOINTED

Dear Child of God,

I know the disappointments of your
heart and desire to be your hope when
you feel as if life has let you down. Trust
Me in the midst of your disappointment,
and believe that I am always looking
out for what's best for you. Remember,
you have not yet reached the end of the
story. So don't be discouraged—I am
still at work creating a beautiful
tapestry in your life.

~God

That is why we never give up. Though our bodies
are dying, our spirits are being renewed every day.
2 CORINTHIANS 4:16 NLT

The Scriptures tell us that no one who
believes in Christ will ever be disappointed.
ROMANS 10:11 TLB

[Be] confident of this, that he who began
a good work in you will carry it on to
completion until the day of Christ Jesus.
PHILIPPIANS 1:6 NIV

As the Scriptures express it, "See, I am sending
Christ to be the carefully chosen, precious
Cornerstone of my church, and I will never
disappoint those who trust in him."
1 PETER 2:6 TLB

Why are you cast down, O my soul?
And *why* are you disquieted within me?
Hope in God, for I shall yet praise Him
For the help of His countenance.
PSALM 42:5 NKJV

This expectation will not disappoint us.
For we know how dearly God loves us,
because he has given us the Holy Spirit
to fill our hearts with his love.
ROMANS 5:5 NLT

*Look upon your chastenings
as God's chariots sent to
carry your soul into the high
places of achievement.*

My Child,

I believe in you. I can see the whole picture while you can see only what is right before you. Lift your head and look to Me. I have an eternal perspective on this temporary situation in your life. The plans I have for you far exceed what you have imagined. I believe in you, so take courage to believe in yourself and in the dreams I have placed in your heart.

~God

O my soul, why be so gloomy and discouraged?
Trust in God! I shall again praise him
for his wondrous help; he will make
me smile again, *for he is my God!*

PSALM 43:5 TLB

Christ, God's faithful Son, is in complete charge of
God's house. And we Christians are God's house—
he lives in us!—if we keep up our courage firm to
the end, and our joy and our trust in the Lord.

HEBREWS 3:6 TLB

I waited patiently *and* expectantly for the Lord;
and He inclined to me and heard my cry.

PSALM 40:1 AMP

Keep up the good work and don't get
discouraged, for you will be rewarded.

2 CHRONICLES 15:7 TLB

Though he stumble, he will not fall,
for the LORD upholds him with his hand.

PSALM 37:24 NIV

Being confident of this very thing, that he
which hath begun a good work in you will
perform *it* until the day of Jesus Christ.

PHILIPPIANS 1:6 KJV

*When we yield to discouragement,
it is usually because we give too
much thought to the past or to the future.*

 # FEARFUL

Beloved,

Do not be afraid because I am with you. Do not give in to the spirit of fear that is so prevalent in the world. Instead, trust Me to love you and care for you daily. You can walk confidently through the battles of life with Me as your powerful ally. Remember My goodness to you in the past, and choose to trust that I will provide for you now—and forever.

~God

Fear thou not; for I *am* with thee: be not dismayed;
for I *am* thy God; I will strengthen thee;
yea, I will help thee; yea, I will uphold thee
with the right hand of my righteousness.
ISAIAH 41:10 KJV

God did not give us a spirit of timidity, but a
spirit of power, of love and of self-discipline.
2 TIMOTHY 1:7 NIV

My flesh and my heart may fail, but God is the Rock
and firm Strength of my heart and my Portion forever.
PSALM 73:26 AMP

Even though I walk through the valley of the
shadow of death, I will fear no evil, for you are
with me; your rod and your staff, they comfort me.
PSALM 23:4 NIV

"Do not fear, for those who are with us
are more than those who are with them."
2 KINGS 6:16 NASB

There is no fear in love. But perfect love drives out
fear, because fear has to do with punishment.
The one who fears is not made perfect in love.
1 JOHN 4:18 NIV

*N*o *coward soul is mine,*
No trembler in the world's
storm-troubled sphere;
I see Heaven's glories shine,
And faith shine equal,
arming me from fear.

GUILTY

Dear One,

My Son, Jesus bore your guilt on the cross when He paid for your sins. You are forgiven and your sins are remembered no more. The hidden sins that darkened your heart are gone, and I have given you a clean heart. You are a new creature in Christ, who will not find condemnation before Me. Please accept My love and grace. See yourself as I do, and enter into the freedom of your redemption.

~God

Now there is no condemnation for
those who belong to Christ Jesus.
ROMANS 8:1 NLT

Create in me a clean heart, O God, and
renew a steadfast spirit within me.
PSALM 51:10 NASB

You, O LORD, keep my lamp burning;
my God turns my darkness into light.
PSALM 18:28 NIV

They sinned against me, but I will wash
away that sin. They did evil and turned
away from me, but I will forgive them.
JEREMIAH 33:8 NCV

Consecrate yourselves therefore, and be holy;
for I am the Lord your God. Keep my statutes,
and observe them; I am the Lord; I sanctify you.
LEVITICUS 20:7-8 NRSV

Christ also loved the church and gave Himself for
her, that He might sanctify and cleanse her with
the washing of water by the word, that He might
present her to Himself a glorious church, not
having spot or wrinkle or any such thing, but
that she should be holy and without blemish.
EPHESIANS 5:25-27 NKJV

*Guilt is the most destructive of all
emotions. It mourns what has been
while playing no part in what
may be, now or in the future.*

JEALOUS

Child of Mine,

Sometimes it is not so much that you envy what others have, but rather what they represent—all the things the world wants you to be. I made you in My image and likeness, so jealousy often signals that you are worshipping something other than Me. Take your eyes off them and look to Me. In My eyes you are growing and are complete in Christ, so see yourself through My eyes. I will help you cleanse your thoughts, renew your heart, and restore a right focus in your life. Allow Me to be the center of your life.

~God

A relaxed attitude lengthens life;
jealousy rots it away.

PROVERBS 14:30 NLT

"I will feast the soul of the priests with
abundance, and my people shall be
satisfied with my goodness," says the LORD.

JEREMIAH 31:14 RSV

Don't envy sinners, but always respect
the Lord. Then you will have hope for the
future, and your wishes will come true.

PROVERBS 23:17-18 NCV

Let your character be free from the love of
money, being content with what you have;
for He Himself has said, "I will never
desert you, nor will I ever forsake you."

HEBREWS 13:5 NASB

Be still before the LORD and wait patiently
for him; do not fret when men succeed in
their ways, when they carry out their wicked
schemes. For evil men will be cut off, but those
who hope in the LORD will inherit the land.

PSALM 37:7, 9 NIV

He satisfies me with good things and
makes me young again, like the eagle.

PSALM 103:5 NCV

*Jealousy contains more of
self-love than of love.*

LONELY

Dear Child of God,

When you feel alone in the world, remember that I am with you and I love you. I will comfort you in every circumstance, as you are My beloved child. Though others reject you, I will not reject you. I accept you and will not abandon you. Allow the times you feel lonely to become gentle reminders to come near to Me and experience My presence in your life.

~God

"Behold, I am with you and will keep you wherever you go, and will bring you back to this land; for I will not leave you until I have done that of which I have spoken to you."

GENESIS 28:15 RSV

Even if my father and mother abandon me, the LORD will hold me close.

PSALM 27:10 NLT

God makes a home for the lonely; He leads out the prisoners into prosperity, Only the rebellious dwell in a parched land.

PSALM 68:6 NASB

I am persuaded that neither death nor life, nor angels nor principalities nor powers, nor things present nor things to come, height nor depth, nor any other created thing, shall be able to separate us from the love of God which is in Christ Jesus our Lord.

ROMANS 8:38-39 NKJV

The eternal God *is thy* refuge, and underneath *are* the everlasting arms.

DEUTERONOMY 33:27 KJV

You are my hiding place; you protect me from trouble. You surround me with songs of victory.

PSALM 32:7 NLT

The best remedy for those who are afraid, lonely, or unhappy, is to go outside somewhere where they can be quiet alone with the heavens, nature, and God.

115

PERSECUTED

My Child,

When you are persecuted for My Name,
you are in good company. Whatever
others have done to you, they have also
done to Me. Forgive them, turn your
hurts over to Me, and allow Me to take
care of you. Entrust the outcome to Me,
for I judge justly. In the end, your
integrity shall uphold you. You are the
apple of My eye, so rejoice in Me, for
My glory rests upon you.

~God

"Blessed are those who have been persecuted for the sake of righteousness, for theirs is the kingdom of heaven. Blessed are you when men revile you and persecute you, and say all kinds of evil against you falsely on account of Me."

MATTHEW 5:10-11 NASB

We have this treasure in earthen vessels, so that the surpassing greatness of the power may be of God and not from ourselves; *we are* afflicted in every way, but not crushed; perplexed, but not despairing; persecuted, but not forsaken; struck down, but not destroyed; always carrying about in the body the dying of Jesus, so that the life of Jesus also may be manifested in our body.

2 CORINTHIANS 4:7-10 NASB

Let all who take refuge in you be glad; let them ever sing for joy. Spread your protection over them, that those who love your name may rejoice in you. For surely, O LORD, you bless the righteous; you surround them with your favor as with a shield.

PSALM 5:11-12 NIV

Love your enemies and pray for those who persecute you

MATTHEW 5:44 NIV

Bless those who persecute you; bless and do not curse.

ROMANS 12:14 NIV

If you are insulted because of the name of Christ, you are blessed, for the Spirit of glory and of God rests on you.

1 PETER 4:14 NIV

Opposition may become sweet to a man when he has christened it persecution.

# PRIDEFUL

Beloved,

Do not think more highly of yourself than you ought, but remember that everything good in you and all the blessings you have are gifts from Me. The world will tell you that you must fight for what is yours and trample others on your way to the top. That is not My way. Listen to My wisdom, and choose the path of humility. The first shall be last and the last shall be first. Trust Me to make a way for you rather than trying to make a way for yourself. Enjoy the privileges of a humble child loved by your adoring Father, and treat others as I treat you.

~God

"He who humbles himself will be exalted."
LUKE 18:14 NKJV

A humble spirit will obtain honor.
PROVERBS 29:23 NASB

The world and everything that people
want in it are passing away, but the person
who does what God wants lives forever.
1 JOHN 2:17 NCV

Whoever becomes simple and elemental again,
like this child, will rank high in God's kingdom.
MATTHEW 18:4 THE MESSAGE

"To the faithful you show yourself faithful, to the
blameless you show yourself blameless, to the pure
you show yourself pure, but to the crooked you
show yourself shrewd. You save the humble, but
the eyes are on the haughty to bring them low."
2 SAMUEL 22:26–28 NIV

Through the grace given to me I say to everyone
among you not to think more highly of
himself than he ought to think; but to
think so as to have sound judgment, as
God has allotted to each a measure of faith.
ROMANS 12:3 NASB

*Our intellect and other gifts have been given
to be used for God's greater glory, but
sometimes they become the very god for us.
That is the saddest part: we are losing
our balance when this happens. We must
free ourselves to be filled by God.
Even God cannot fill what is full.*

STRESSED

Dear One,

Don't fill your plate so full. You don't have to please everyone. It's okay to say no. You can find the quietness and peace you need by trusting in Me and letting Me care for you. Choose the most treasured things to fill your plate, and then take time to enjoy them. Live your life with an eternal rhythm instead of living by the clock. Abide in Me, and I'll give you my peace. Remember, unless the Lord builds the house, they labor in vain who build it.

~God

"Come to Me, all *you* who labor and are
heavy laden, and I will give you rest."

MATTHEW 11:28 NKJV

Cast your burden upon the LORD, and
He will sustain you; He will never
allow the righteous to be shaken.

PSALM 55:22 NASB

You will keep in perfect peace him whose mind is
steadfast, because he trusts in you. Trust in the LORD
forever, for the LORD, the LORD, is the Rock eternal.

ISAIAH 26:3-4 NIV

Consider the blameless, observe the upright;
there is a future for the man of peace.

PSALM 37:37 NIV

The peace of God, which passeth all understanding,
shall keep your hearts and minds through Christ Jesus.

PHILIPPIANS 4:7 KJV

Those who trust in, lean on, *and* confidently hope
in the Lord are like Mount Zion, which cannot
be moved but abides *and* stands fast forever.

PSALM 125:1 AMP

*One of the best ways to
counteract stress is to
pray for others.*

TEMPTED

Child of Mine,

When temptation knocks at your door, don't answer. It may offer a shortcut to your dreams, but there is a high price to pay. I am your strength when you are weak. Look to Me as your tower of strength to resist temptation, and take My hand and follow Me away from it. I will restore your faith and give you courage to overcome temptation so that your heart may continually please Me.

~God

No temptation has overtaken you that is not common to man. God is faithful, and he will not let you be tempted beyond your strength, but with the temptation will also provide the way of escape, that you may be able to endure it.

1 CORINTHIANS 10:13 RSV

Since he himself has now been through suffering and temptation, he knows what it is like when we suffer and are tempted, and he is wonderfully able to help us.

HEBREWS 2:18 TLB

We do not have a High Priest who cannot sympathize with our weaknesses, but was in all *points* tempted as *we are, yet* without sin. Let us therefore come boldly to the throne of grace, that we may obtain mercy and find grace to help in time of need.

HEBREWS 4:15–16 NKJV

Blessed, happy, to be envied is the man who is patient under trial *and* stands up under temptation, for when he has stood the test *and* been approved he will receive [the victor's] crown of life which God has promised to those who love Him.

JAMES 1:12 AMP

Put on the whole armor of God, that you may be able to stand against the wiles of the devil.

EPHESIANS 6:11 NKJV

People who love the LORD hate evil. . . . and [He] frees them from the power of the wicked.

PSALM 97:10 NCV

Our lives and eternal souls
are in the hands that
were nailed to the Cross.

123

 WORRIED

Dear Child of God,

I know you are busy with your life and all the things so many depend on you to do. However, don't become distracted with so much serving that you forget to spend time with Me. Of all the things you consider as needs in your life that worry you, only one thing is most important—your time with Me. When you make time for Me, I will make time for all the really important things. I will show you what is necessary and what to leave behind in your day. Walk through your day with Me—and don't worry so much!

~God

I was very worried, but you comforted
me and made me happy.

PSALM 94:19 NCV

[Cast] all your anxiety on Him,
because He cares for you.

1 PETER 5:7 NASB

The fear of the LORD leads to life; then one
rests content, untouched by trouble.

PROVERBS 19:23 NIV

"But seek first His kingdom and His righteousness,
and all these things will be added to you.
Therefore do not worry about tomorrow;
for tomorrow will care for itself."

MATTHEW 6:33-34 NASB

God is greater than our worried hearts and
knows more about us than we do ourselves.

1 JOHN 3:20 THE MESSAGE

Anxiety weighs down the human heart,
but a good word cheers it up.

PROVERBS 12:25 NRSV

*Worry is interest paid on trouble
before it falls due.*

GOD'S
PROMISES
CONCERNING . . .

DISCIPLINE

My Child,

My discipline brings life, for in the end it produces righteousness and Christ-like character in you. It is not out of anger toward you, but out of compassionate care for you, for I have your best in mind. Remember, those I love I discipline so that they will share My holiness. So submit yourself to Me. Let Me make you strong and build substance in you. It will pay eternal dividends in your life, both now and forever.

~God

Blessed is the man whom God corrects; so do
not despise the discipline of the Almighty.
JOB 5:17 NIV

Happy are those whom you discipline, LORD.
PSALM 94:12 NLT

"I am with you and will save you," declares the LORD.
"Though I completely destroy all the nations among
which I scatter you, I will not completely destroy
you. I will discipline you but only with justice."
JEREMIAH 30:11 NIV

No discipline is enjoyable while it is
happening—it is painful! But afterward
there will be a quiet harvest of right living
for those who are trained in this way.
HEBREWS 12:11 NLT

In all these things we overwhelmingly
conquer through Him who loved us.
ROMANS 8:37 NASB

"My son, don't be angry when the Lord punishes
you. Don't be discouraged when he has to
show you where you are wrong. For when he
punishes you, it proves that he loves you."
HEBREWS 12:5-6 TLB

*Everyone wants to change, but change
demands desire and discipline before
it becomes delightful. There is
always the agony of choice
before the promise of change.*

FAITHFULNESS

Beloved,

I assure you that I will be faithful to be there for you. I am with you in times of trouble and in times of peace. I will go with you, shelter you from the storm, and strengthen you with my right hand. Don't be afraid of what lies ahead, for My faithful presence will be there with you. I am able to protect you and keep you. When you ask, I will answer. When you speak, I will listen. I am faithful throughout eternity to be your companion.

~God

The LORD passed in front of Moses and said,
"I am the LORD. The LORD is a God who shows
mercy, who is kind, who doesn't become angry
quickly, who has great love and faithfulness."

EXODUS 34:6 NCV

All the paths of the LORD are steadfast
love and faithfulness, for those who
keep his covenant and his testimonies.

PSALM 25:10 RSV

Your unfailing love will last forever.
Your faithfulness is as enduring as the heavens.

PSALM 89:2 NLT

O LORD, thou *art* my God; I will exalt thee,
I will praise thy name; for thou hast done
wonderful *things; thy* counsels of old
are faithfulness *and* truth.

ISAIAH 25:1 KJV

Hear my prayer, O Lord, give ear to
my supplications! In Your faithfulness
answer me, and in Your righteousness.

PSALM 143:1 AMP

He will cover you with His pinions,
And under His wings you may seek refuge;
His faithfulness is a shield and bulwark.

PSALM 91:4 NASB

I do not pray for success,
I ask for faithfulness.

FORGIVENESS

Dear One,

I offer My forgiveness freely to you.
When your heart is heavy because of
what you have done—and because of
what you left undone—I will forgive
you. I will never turn you away but
instead will cleanse you and give you
mercy to begin anew. I will remove
your shame and sadness and fill you
with a new joy. All you have to do is
ask Me. I am here—waiting.

~God

He is faithful and just to forgive us *our* sins
and to cleanse us from all unrighteousness.

1 JOHN 1:9 NKJV

In him we have redemption through his blood,
the forgiveness of our trespasses, according to the
riches of his grace which he lavished upon us.

EPHESIANS 1:7-8 RSV

As far as the east is from the west,
So far has He removed our transgressions from us.

PSALM 103:12 NASB

"Come now, let us reason together," says the Lord:
"though your sins are like scarlet, they shall
be as white as snow; though they are red
like crimson, they shall become like wool."

ISAIAH 1:18 RSV

Our God, no one is like you. We are all
that is left of your chosen people, and you
freely forgive our sin and guilt. You don't stay
angry forever; you're glad to have pity.

MICAH 7:18 CEV

[The LORD declares:] "I, I am the One
who forgives all your sins, for my sake;
I will not remember your sins."

ISAIAH 43:25 NCV

*F*orgiveness is like faith.
You have to keep reviving it.

FRIENDSHIP

Child of Mine,

I want you to have friends who will love and honor you just as you love and honor them. I will bring these quality friendships into your life. Love them as you love Me. Give yourself to them sacrificially, not only looking after your own interest but also looking after their best interests. I will knit your hearts together as you include Me in your relationships. Appreciate these friendships I bring your way for they are for your blessing and happiness.

~God

Share each other's troubles and problems,
and in this way obey the law of Christ.

GALATIANS 6:2 NLT

A man *who has* friends must himself
be friendly, but there is a friend
who sticks closer than a brother.

PROVERBS 18:24 NKJV

Whoever loves his brother [believer] abides (lives)
in the Light, and in It *or* in him there is no
occasion for stumbling *or* cause for error *or* sin.

1 JOHN 2:10 AMP

The pleasantness of one's friend springs
from his earnest counsel.

PROVERBS 27:9 NIV

A friend is always loyal, and a brother
is born to help in time of need.

PROVERBS 17:17 NLT

I call you not servants; for the servant knoweth
not what his lord doeth: but I have called you
friends; for all things that I have heard of
my Father I have made known unto you.

JOHN 15:15 KJV

*Friendship is a serious affection;
the most sublime of all affections,
because it is founded on principle
and cemented by time.*

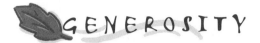# GENEROSITY

Dear Child of God,

I have given you many gifts and talents, and I have blessed you so that you have the ability and privilege to bless others. When you give of yourself, you are pleasing Me with your generosity. When you open your hand, you express My love to the world.

~God

God has given gifts to each of you from his
great variety of spiritual gifts. Manage them well
so that God's generosity can flow through you.

1 PETER 4:10 NLT

Who am I and who are my people that we
should be able to offer as generously as this?
For all things come from Thee, and
from Thy hand we have given Thee.

1 CHRONICLES 29:14 NASB

Good will come to him who is generous and lends
freely, who conducts his affairs with justice.

PSALM 112:5 NIV

You will be made rich in every way so that you can
be generous on every occasion, and through us
your generosity will result in thanksgiving to God.

2 CORINTHIANS 9:11 NIV

A generous man will himself be blessed,
for he shares his food with the poor.

PROVERBS 22:9 NIV

Command them to do good, to be rich in good
deeds, and to be generous and willing to share.
In this way they will lay up treasure for themselves
as a firm foundation for the coming age, so that
they may take hold of the life that is truly life.

1 TIMOTHY 6:18-19 NIV

*Indulge yourself and you are bound
to find emptiness. Give of yourself
and you will always find happiness.*

GENTLENESS

My Child,

My gentleness makes you great. Let My
meekness create in you a spirit of
gentleness. For what this world needs is
the gentle touch of My love through
your life. Combine gentle words with
kind acts that reveal My goodness for
those around you. Treat them with the
gentleness with which I treat you.

~God

The meek will inherit the land and enjoy great peace.
PSALM 37:11 NIV

You have given me the shield of your salvation;
your gentleness has made me great.
2 SAMUEL 22:36 TLB

Pursue righteousness, godliness, faith, love,
endurance and gentleness. Fight the good fight
of the faith. Take hold of the eternal life to
which you were called when you made your good
confession in the presence of many witnesses.
1 TIMOTHY 6:11–12 NIV

When the Holy Spirit controls our lives he
will produce this kind of fruit in us: love,
joy, peace, patience, kindness, goodness,
faithfulness, gentleness and self-control.
GALATIANS 5:22–23 TLB

Which do you want: that I come to you with
punishment or with love and gentleness?
1 CORINTHIANS 4:21 NCV

Let everyone see that you are gentle
and kind. The Lord is coming soon.
PHILIPPIANS 4:5 NCV

*Children learn to care by experiencing
good care. They come to know
the blessings of gentleness . . .
through the way in which
they themselves are treated.*

Beloved,

I desire to share all that I am with you—pouring out My goodness, kindness, good gifts, and blessings upon you. I watch over you with great love and appreciate it when you express your gratitude for My care. Allow Me to love you. I am always there for you. I will fill you with more peace, love, and joy until you overflow.

~God

Thanks be to God, who gives us the victory
through our Lord Jesus Christ.

1 CORINTHIANS 15:57 NASB

Let your roots grow down into him and draw up
nourishment from him. See that you go on growing
in the Lord, and become strong and vigorous in
the truth you were taught. Let your lives overflow
with joy and thanksgiving for all he has done.

COLOSSIANS 2:7 TLB

I urge, then, first of all, that requests, prayers,
intercession and thanksgiving be made for everyone—
for kings and all those in authority, that we may live
peaceful and quiet lives in all godliness and holiness.

1 TIMOTHY 2:1-2 NIV

Therefore, since we receive a kingdom which cannot be
shaken, let us show gratitude, by which we may offer
to God an acceptable service with reverence and awe.

HEBREWS 12:28 NASB

Give the coat back at sunset, because your
neighbor needs that coat to sleep in, and he
will be grateful to you. And the Lord your
God will see that you have done a good thing.

DEUTERONOMY 24:13 NCV

Let the word of Christ dwell in you richly;
teach and admonish one another in all wisdom;
and with gratitude in your hearts sing psalms,
hymns, and spiritual songs to God.

COLOSSIANS 3:16 NRSV

For each new morning with its light,
Father, we thank thee.
For rest and shelter of the night,
Father, we thank thee.
For health and food, for love and friends,
For everything thy goodness sends,
Father in heaven, we thank thee.

141

# HEAVEN

Dear One,

When you have completed all that I have for you to do on earth, then you will join Me in Heaven. I have a place prepared for you when it is time for you to come to Me, and it is filled with many treasures. It is My home, and I want to share it with you for eternity. There are many things close to My heart that I will share with you — things that cannot be revealed at this time, but are reserved for you in Heaven. I love you, and I love spending time with you, on earth now, and in the days to come, in Heaven.

~God

We know that when this earthly tent we live in is
taken down—when we die and leave these bodies—
we will have a home in heaven, an eternal body
made for us by God himself and not by human hands.

2 CORINTHIANS 5:1 NLT

"There are many rooms in my Father's house;
I would not tell you this if it were not true.
I am going there to prepare a place for you."

JOHN 14:2 NCV

"Rejoice and be glad, because great
is your reward in heaven."

MATTHEW 5:12 NIV

This world is not our home; we are looking forward
to our city in heaven, which is yet to come.

HEBREWS 13:14 NLT

"Do not lay up for yourselves treasures on earth,
where moth and rust destroy, and where thieves break
in and lay. But store up for yourselves treasures in
heaven, where neither moth nor rust destroys, and
where thieves do not break in or steal; for where
your treasure is, there will your heart be also."

MATTHEW 6:19-21 NASB

Blessed *be* the God and Father of our Lord Jesus
Christ, who according to His abundant mercy has
begotten us again to a living hope through the
resurrection of Jesus Christ from the dead, to an
inheritance incorruptible and undefiled and that
does not fade away, reserved in heaven for you,
who are kept by the power of God through faith for
salvation ready to be revealed in the last time.

1 PETER 1:3-5 NKJV

*Heaven is large and affords space for
all modes of love and fortitude.*

Child of Mine,

I have given you life abundantly through Christ Jesus. His blood sealed the covenant between us. Through Christ, all the blessings I promised in the covenant with Him belong to you. I will bless you, prosper you, and defend you. All I ask of you is that you obey My commands—love Me with all your heart, mind, and soul, and love your neighbor as yourself. I will open up heavenly storehouses and bless your life. I am your God, and you are my beloved child.

~God

"I will establish My covenant between Me and you
and your descendants after you throughout their
generations for an everlasting covenant, to be
God to you and to your descendants after you."
GENESIS 17:7 NASB

If ye *be* Christ's, then are ye Abraham's seed,
and heirs according to the promise.
GALATIANS 3:29 KJV

"Then I will keep my covenant with
them and take away their sins."
ROMANS 11:27 NLT

From everlasting to everlasting the LORD's love is
with those who fear him, and his righteousness
with their children's children—with those who keep
his covenant and remember to obey his precepts.
PSALM 103:17-18 NIV

"I will look on you favorably and make you fruitful,
multiply you and confirm My covenant with you."
LEVITICUS 26:9 NKJV

You must completely obey the LORD your God,
and you must carefully follow all his commands
I am giving you today. Then the LORD your God
will make you greater than any other nation
on earth. Obey the LORD your God so that all
these blessings will come and stay with you.
DEUTERONOMY 28:1-2 NCV

*This is my blood of the
covenant, which is
poured out for many.*

145

HIS PRESENCE

Dear Child of God,

I am with you always. My presence will go with you every day. Come and sit with Me, and experience sweet fellowship—for in My presence is fullness of joy. I find it so refreshing when you rest in My arms after a weary day. In My presence you will find the peace you're looking for. I have everything you need; so come to Me, and allow Me to fill you with all that I am.

~God

Your ears will hear a word behind you,
"This is the way, walk in it," whenever
you turn to the right or to the left.

ISAIAH 30:21 NASB

"Remember, your Father knows exactly
what you need even before you ask him!"

MATTHEW 6:8 TLB

"Where two or three have gathered together
in My name, there I am in their midst."

MATTHEW 18:20 NASB

My presence shall go *with thee*,
and I will give thee rest.

EXODUS 33:14 ASV

"Be sure of this—that I am with you always,
even to the end of the world."

MATTHEW 28:20 TLB

I cried out to the LORD in my suffering, and
he heard me. He set me free from all my fears.
For the angel of the LORD guards all
who fear him, and he rescues them.

PSALM 34:6-7 NLT

*Henceforth I learn that to obey is best,
And love with fear the only God, to walk
As in his presence, ever to observe
His providence, and on
him sole depend.*

HIS WORD

My Child,

Allow My Word to be a lamp unto your feet and a light unto your path. With it you will never be in darkness, for it will light your way. My Word will never pass away; you can count on the promises I make for eternity. It will not fail you, but it will accomplish all that it is sent forth to do. My Word is established forever. Put it into your heart so that you can become strong and secure in Me. Then do what it says, so that your life will reflect my power.

~God

"It is written in the Scriptures, 'A person
does not live by eating only bread,
but by everything God says.'"

MATTHEW 4:4 NCV

Blessed are they that hear the
word of God, and keep it.

LUKE 11:28 ASV

"Heaven and earth shall disappear,
but my words stand sure forever."

MARK 13:31 TLB

Thy word is a lamp unto my feet,
And light unto my path.

PSALM 119:105 ASV

Do what God's teaching says; when you only listen
and do nothing, you are fooling yourselves.

JAMES 1:22 NCV

The word of God *is* living and powerful, and
sharper than any two-edged sword, piercing
even to the division of soul and spirit, and
of joints and marrow, and is a discerner of
the thoughts and intents of the heart.

HEBREWS 4:12 NKJV

*A reformation happens every time
you open the Bible.*

HONOR

Beloved,

When you honor Me, I will honor you.
When you seek My face and do My Word,
you bring honor to Me. And those who
follow Me and serve Me will receive My
honor. Call upon Me. I will answer you;
I will be with you in trouble. I will
deliver you and honor you.

~God

My mouth shall be filled with Your praise
and with Your honor all the day.

PSALM 71:8 AMP

Keep traveling steadily along [the Lord's]
pathway and in due season he will
honor you with every blessing.

PSALM 37:34 TLB

He will call upon me, and I will answer him;
I will be with him in trouble,
I will deliver him and honor him.

PSALM 91:15 NIV

You have made him a little lower than the angels,
And You have crowned him with glory and honor.

PSALM 8:5 NKJV

Honor the Lord by giving him the first part
of all your income, and he will fill your
barns with wheat and barley and overflow
your wine vats with the finest wines.

PROVERBS 3:9 TLB

[Jesus said,] "Whoever serves me must follow me;
and where I am, my servant also will be.
My Father will honor the one who serves me."

JOHN 12:26 NIV

Who sows virtue reaps honor.

INTEGRITY

Dear One,

The world tells you that prosperity comes to those who aggressively seek advancement, no matter what the cost. I say to you, walk before Me with integrity of heart, doing all that I have asked of you. As you keep My commandments, I will establish you. Live a life of integrity, and you will be secure in all you do. Do not seek public acclaim or wealth, but rather to serve Me and those I call you to with integrity of heart. For there you will find true riches.

~God

He who walks in integrity walks securely.

PROVERBS 10:9 RSV

As for you, if you will walk before me, as David your father walked, with integrity of heart and uprightness, doing according to all that I have commanded you, and keeping my statutes and my ordinances, then I will establish your royal throne over Israel for ever, as I promised.

1 KINGS 9:4-5 RSV

By standing firm you will gain life.

LUKE 21:19 NIV

The integrity of the upright will guide them.

PROVERBS 11:3 NASB

May integrity and honesty protect me, for I put my hope in you.

PSALM 25:21 NLT

In my integrity you uphold me and set me in your presence forever.

PSALM 41:12 NIV

To starve to death is a small thing, but to lose one's integrity is a great one.

153

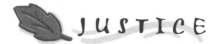

JUSTICE

Child of Mine,

Walk justly, but do not judge. It is not for you to judge or take revenge on those who mistreat you. Rather, I call you to entrust yourself to Me, for I am the One who judges justly. And I will take care of you. When you are unjustly treated and do right, you honor Me by not retaliating. You act like My Son, for He did not open His mouth in retaliation, but entrusted Himself to Me. In the end, you will see justice served. Fear not. I will help you.

~God

He is the Rock, His work is perfect, for all His ways
are law *and* justice. A God of faithfulness without
breach *or* deviation, just and right is He.
DEUTERONOMY 32:4 AMP

God presented him as a sacrifice of atonement,
through faith in his blood. He did this to
demonstrate his justice, because in his forbearance
he had left the sins committed beforehand
unpunished—he did it to demonstrate his justice
at the present time, so as to be just and the one
who justifies those who have faith in Jesus.
ROMANS 3:25-26 NIV

Justice, *and only* justice, you shall pursue,
that you may live and possess the land
which the LORD your God is giving you.
DEUTERONOMY 16:20 NASB

Then my enemies will retreat in the day when
I call. This I know, that God is for me.
PSALM 56:9 NRSV

Morning by morning [the Lord] dispenses his
justice, and every new day he does not fail.
ZEPHANIAH 3:5 NIV

"Behold, all those who were incensed against you
Shall be ashamed and disgraced;
They shall be as nothing, And those
who strive with you shall perish. . . .
For I, the LORD your God, will hold your right hand,
Saying to you, 'Fear not, I will help you.'"
ISAIAH 41:11-13 NKJV

*J*ustice consists in doing no injury to men;
decency in giving them no offence.

155

KINDNESS

Dear Child of God,

My heart is forever turned toward you.
With an everlasting kindness, I will
have mercy on you; and I will show you
My marvelous love. I stand ready to
pardon all who ask for forgiveness. I
will never forsake those who come to
Me. Seek Me with all your heart, and
let Me fill you with My Spirit. Let My
goodness and kindness fill your life
with salvation, healing, and love.

~God

Give thanks to the LORD, for He is good;
for His lovingkindness is everlasting.
PSALM 118:1 NASB

His merciful kindness is great toward us.
PSALM 117:2 KJV

The kindness and the love of God our Savior toward
man appeared, not by works of righteousness
which we have done, but according to His mercy
He saved us, through the washing of regeneration
and renewing of the Holy Spirit.
TITUS 3:4-5 NKJV

In a little burst of wrath I hid My face from you
for a moment, but with age-enduring love *and*
kindness I will have compassion *and* mercy
on you, says the Lord, your Redeemer.
ISAIAH 54:8 AMP

They refused to obey, and were not mindful of the
wonders that you performed among them; but they
stiffened their necks and determined to return to their
slavery in Egypt. But you are a God ready to forgive,
gracious and merciful, slow to anger and abounding
in steadfast love, and you did not forsake them.
NEHEMIAH 9:17 NRSV

Praise the LORD. His love to me was wonderful
when my city was attacked. In my distress, I said,
"God cannot see me!" But you heard my prayer
when I cried out to you for help.
PSALM 31:21-22 NCV

*S*pread love everywhere you go: First of
all in your own house... let no one ever
come to you without leaving better and
happier. Be the living expression of
God's kindness; kindness in your face,
kindness in your eyes, kindness in your
smile, kindness in your warm greeting.

157

LOVE

My Child,

I have loved you with an everlasting love. I love you so much that I call you My very own child. I gave My only begotten Son for you that you may have eternal life and fellowship with Me forever. Love never stops, but selflessly puts others first. Love doesn't force itself on others and say, "Look at me!" Love is even tempered. It doesn't keep score. Love always trusts. Love never looks back but steps up and presses on to the end. I am love. And when you choose to dwell in Me, I shall love others through you.

~God

Most important of all, continue to show deep love for each other, for love makes up for many of your faults.
1 PETER 4:8 TLB

Most important, love each other. Love is what holds you all together in perfect unity.
COLOSSIANS 3:14 NCV

Many sorrows come to the wicked, but abiding love surrounds those who trust in the Lord.
PSALM 32:10 TLB

There are three things that will endure—faith, hope, and love—and the greatest of these is love.
1 CORINTHIANS 13:13 NLT

If you love someone you will be loyal to him no matter what the cost. You will always believe in him, always expect the best of him, and always stand your ground in defending him.
1 CORINTHIANS 13:7 TLB

May the Lord make your love increase and overflow for each other and for everyone else, just as ours does for you.
1 THESSALONIANS 3:12 NIV

Love feels no burden, thinks nothing of trouble, attempts what is above its strength, pleads no excuse of impossibility; for it thinks all things lawful for itself, and all things possible. It is therefore able to undertake all things, and warrants them to take effect, where he who does not love, would faint and lie down.

159

MERCY

Beloved,

My mercies are new every morning. I surround you with My love, compassion, and kindness. I am faithfully near you. When you cry out for help, I answer. I have saved you from sin. On the most difficult days you will find strength to stand strong in My loving embrace. Weeping may endure for a night, but joy comes in the morning. My compassion will not fail you, so hold tightly to Me. I am your merciful Father.

~God

The LORD is kind and shows mercy. He does not become angry quickly but is full of love. The LORD is good to everyone; he is merciful to all he has made.

PSALM 145:8-9 NCV

Since then we have a great high priest who has passed through the heavens, Jesus the Son of God, let us hold fast our confession. For we do not have a high priest who cannot sympathize with our weaknesses, but one who has been tempted in all things as *we are, yet* without sin. Let us therefore draw near with confidence to the throne of grace, so that we may receive mercy and find grace to help in time of need.

HEBREWS 4:14-16 NASB

His mercy extends to those who fear him, from generation to generation.

LUKE 1:50 NIV

The Lord our God is merciful and forgiving.

DANIEL 9:9 NIV

"Because of God's tender mercy, the light from heaven is about to break upon us, to give light to those who sit in darkness and in the shadow of death, and to guide us to the path of peace."

LUKE 1:78-79 NLT

Sow to yourselves in righteousness, reap in mercy; break up your fallow ground: for *it is* time to seek the LORD, till he come and rain righteousness upon you.

HOSEA 10:12 KJV

There's a wideness in God's mercy,
Like the wideness of the sea;
There's a kindness in his justice,
Which is more than liberty.

PRAYER

Dear One,

Communication with you is important to My relationship with you. I love it when you talk to Me about your life, your hopes, and your dreams. Pray without ceasing, for I am always here to listen and respond to your prayers. I enjoy the time you spend with Me in prayer—earnest prayer for a need you have, prayers of thanksgiving and praise, and the times when you simply want to talk to Me. You can pray at any time. You don't need an invitation or a formal occasion to pray. Just come to Me; I am always here waiting for you.

~God

Jesus told his disciples a parable to show them
that they should always pray and not give up.

PSALM/LUKE **18:1** NIV

In every thing by prayer and supplication
with thanksgiving let your requests
be made known unto God.

PHILIPPIANS **4:6** KJV

The earnest prayer of a righteous person
has great power and wonderful results.

JAMES **5:16** NLT

My voice shalt thou hear in the morning,
O LORD; in the morning will I direct *my
prayer* unto thee, and will look up.

PSALM **5:3** KJV

While Jesus lived on earth, he prayed to God and
asked God for help. He prayed with loud cries and
tears to the One who could save him from death,
and his prayer was heard because he trusted God.

HEBREWS **5:7** NCV

"And everything you ask in prayer,
believing, you will receive."

MATTHEW **21:22** NASB

I *have never been disappointed
when I asked in a humble and
sincere way for God's help.
I pray often.*

Child of Mine,

As I have forgiven you, now you must forgive others. I have reconciled you to myself through Jesus' death, burial, and resurrection. And through My great mercy and love you, too, can forgive others and reconcile with them. I have given you the ability to love them. I have poured out My own love in your heart so that you might love them with My love. You can do it. I will help you. Step out in faith and I will meet you.

~God

If while we were enemies we were reconciled to God through the death of His son, much more, having been reconciled, we shall be saved by His life. And not only this, but we also exult in God through our Lord Jesus Christ, through whom we have now received the reconciliation.

ROMANS 5:10-11 NASB

Be kind and compassionate to one another, forgiving each other, just as in Christ God forgave you.

EPHESIANS 4:32 NIV

Christ God was reconciling the world to himself, not counting their trespasses against them, and entrusting the message of reconciliation to us.

2 CORINTHIANS 5:19 NRSV

"Rebuke your brother if he sins, and forgive him if he is sorry."

LUKE 17:3 TLB

It was the *Father's* good pleasure for all the fulness to dwell in Him, and through Him to reconcile all things to Himself, having made peace through the blood of His cross; through Him, *I say,* whether things on earth or things in heaven.

COLOSSIANS 1:19-20 NASB

He Himself is our peace, who has made both one, and has broken down the middle wall of separation, having abolished in His flesh the enmity, *that is,* the law of commandments *contained* in ordinances, so as to create in Himself one new man *from* the two, *thus* making peace.

EPHESIANS 2:14-16 NKJV

Christ comes to bind lives to God through reconciliation. He comes to bind human lives closely to one another in fellowship. He comes to bind up the individual human life that is lost and divided. Christian unity involves all three of these aspects of peace.

RELATIONSHIPS

Dear Child of God,

I want your relationships with others to reflect your relationship with Me. I am loving, gentle, merciful, and kind— and so should you be. When you forgive others, encourage others, and appreciate their individuality, your life is a reflection of the way I have treated you. When people look at you, I want them to see Me through you. As you grow, build lasting relationships by following My example. I will help you relate to others with a pure heart if you will come to Me for help.

~God

Oil and perfume rejoice the heart;
so does the sweetness of a friend's
counsel that comes from the heart.

PROVERBS 27:9 AMP

Greater love hath no man than this, that
a man lay down his life for his friends.

JOHN 15:13 KJV

Now you can have real love for everyone
because your souls have been cleansed from
selfishness and hatred when you trusted Christ
to save you; so see to it that you really do
love each other warmly, with all your hearts.

1 PETER 1:22 TLB

Share each other's troubles and problems,
and in this way obey the law of Christ.

GALATIANS 6:2 NLT

Never abandon a friend—either yours or your
father's. Then you won't need to go to a
distant relative for help in your time of need.

PROVERBS 27:10 TLB

Two people can accomplish more than twice as
much as one; they get a better return for their
labor. If one person falls, the other can reach out
and help. But people who are alone when they fall
are in real trouble. And on a cold night, two under
the same blanket can gain warmth from each other.
But how can one be warm alone? A person standing
alone can be attacked and defeated, but two can
stand back-to-back and conquer. Three are even
better, for a triple-braided cord is not easily broken.

ECCLESIASTES 4:9-12 NLT

*If we would build on a sure foundation
in friendship, we must love our friends
for their sakes rather than our own.*

RIGHTEOUSNESS

My Child,

I watch as you live upright before Me. Your right-standing with Me is not earned or a result of what you have done, but what Jesus did from the Cross to the Resurrection. I counted you righteous when you accepted Him. I still do. And I have given you My Spirit so that your righteous position will progressively become your life's practice. For I call you to live what you are. In doing that, you will find great joy, and your life will witness that you belong to Me.

~God

"Blessed are those who are persecuted
for righteousness, for the kingdom
of heaven belongs to them."

MATTHEW 5:10 NET

When the storm has swept by, the wicked are gone,
but the righteous stand firm forever.

PROVERBS 10:25 NIV

You bless the godly man, O Lord;
you protect him with your shield of love.

PSALM 5:12 TLB

Riches gotten by doing wrong have no value,
but right living will save you from death.

PROVERBS 10:2 NCV

Your riches won't help you on Judgment Day;
only righteousness counts then.

PROVERBS 11:4 TLB

The LORD is my shepherd, I shall not be in want. He
makes me lie down in green pastures, he leads me
beside quiet waters, he restores my soul. He guides
me in the paths of righteousness for his name's sake.

PSALM 23:1-3 NIV

*Truth and kindness in sweet embrace
Righteousness and peace are God's grace;
For truth out of the
earth does spring,
And righteousness
from heaven ring.*

169

TRUST

Beloved,

Trust Me with your life and all that concerns you, for I love you completely and want to lead you down the path of life. I rescued you from darkness and brought you into the light. I will protect you and will not allow you to be disgraced, for I am your strength and shield from danger. I am able to deliver you out of all your troubles. I sent My Son to give you life abundant and eternal. With Him, I will freely give you all the good things that I have promised you in My Word. Will you trust Me?

~God

Trust in the LORD with all your heart and
lean not on your own understanding;
in all your ways acknowledge him,
and he will make your paths straight

PROVERBS 3:5-6 NIV

Those who know your name trust in you,
for you, O LORD, have never abandoned
anyone who searches for you.

PSALM 9:10 NLT

He who trusts in the LORD will prosper.

PROVERBS 28:25 NIV

Blessed are *all* those who put their trust in Him.

PSALM 2:12 NKJV

In God I have put my trust, I shall not be afraid.

PSALM 56:11 NASB

It is better to trust the LORD than to trust people.

PSALM 118:8 NCV

*Having thus chosen our course,
without guile and with pure
purpose, let us renew our trust in
God and go forward without fear.*

TRUTH

Dear One,

Don't look for easy answers from those who tell you what you want to hear. Follow My path, for I have called you to live in truth. Love the truth, and purify yourself by obeying it. Seek the truth, and follow it passionately, for the way of truth leads to life everlasting. For My truth sets you free.

~God

Jesus said to them, "I am the way, and the truth,
and the life; no one comes to the Father
but through Me. If you had known Me, you
would have known My Father also; from now
on you know Him, and have seen Him."

JOHN 14:6-7 NASB

Now that you have purified yourselves by obeying
the truth so that you have sincere love for your
brothers, love one another deeply, from the heart.

1 PETER 1:22-23 NIV

Love does not delight in evil but
rejoices with the truth.

1 CORINTHIANS 13:6 NIV

"When he, the Spirit of truth comes,
he will guide you into all truth."

JOHN 16:13 NIV

Meanwhile, we've got our hands full continually
thanking God for you, our good friends—so loved by
God! God picked you out as his from the very start.
Think of it: included in God's original plan of
salvation by the bond of faith in the living truth.

2 THESSALONIANS 2:13 THE MESSAGE

Behold, You desire truth in the inner being; make
me therefore to know wisdom in my inmost heart.

PSALM 51:6 AMP

*Truth is always in harmony with herself and
is not concerned chiefly to reveal the justice
that may consist with wrong-doing.*

Child of Mine,

Work hard and cheerfully in all that you do as though you were working for Me and not for those in leadership over you. Remember that I am the one who will give you your reward—not them. Work cheerfully and diligently for Me, and I will bless the work of your hands and reward you with the rich inheritance that I have reserved and prepared for you.

~God

God has promised us a Sabbath when we
will rest, even though it has not yet come.
On that day God's people will rest from
their work, just as God rested from his work.

HEBREWS 4:9-10 CEV

Servants, respectfully obey your earthly masters but
always with an eye to obeying the real master, Christ.
Don't just do what you have to do to get by, but work
heartily, as Christ's servants doing what God wants
you to do. And work with a smile on your face,
always keeping in mind that no matter who happens
to be giving the orders, you're really serving God.

EPHESIANS 6:5-7 THE MESSAGE

Work hard and cheerfully at all you do, just as
though you were working for the Lord and not
merely for your masters, remembering that
it is the Lord Christ who is going to pay you,
giving you your full portion of all he owns.
He is the one you are really working for.

COLOSSIANS 3:23-24 TLB

Study to shew thyself approved unto God,
a workman that needeth not to be ashamed,
rightly dividing the word of truth.

2 TIMOTHY 2:15 KJV

Whatever work you do, do your best.

ECCLESIASTES 9:10 NCV

His master said to him, "Well done, good and
trustworthy slave; you have been trustworthy in a
few things, I will put you in charge of many
things; enter into the joy of your master."

MATTHEW 25:23 NRSV

*It is not only prayer that
gives God glory but work.*

READ THROUGH THE BIBLE IN ONE YEAR

JANUARY

1. Genesis 1-2; Psalm 1; Matthew 1-2
2. Genesis 3-4; Psalm 2; Matthew 3-4
3. Genesis 5-7; Psalm 3; Matthew 5
4. Genesis 8-9; Psalm 4; Matthew 6-7
5. Genesis 10-11; Psalm 5; Matthew 8-9
6. Genesis 12-13; Psalm 6; Matthew 10-11
7. Genesis 14-15; Psalm 7; Matthew 12
8. Genesis 16-17; Psalm 8; Matthew 13
9. Genesis 18-19; Psalm 9; Matthew 14-15
10. Genesis 20-21; Psalm 10; Matthew 16-17
11. Genesis 22-23; Psalm 11; Matthew 18
12. Genesis 24; Psalm 12; Matthew 19-20
13. Genesis 25-26; Psalm 13; Matthew 21
14. Genesis 27-28; Psalm 14; Matthew 22
15. Genesis 29-30; Psalm 15; Matthew 23
16. Genesis 31-32; Psalm 16; Matthew 24
17. Genesis 33-34; Psalm 17; Matthew 25
18. Genesis 35-36; Psalm 18; Matthew 26
19. Genesis 37-38; Psalm 19; Matthew 27
20. Genesis 39-40; Psalm 20; Matthew 28
21. Genesis 41-42; Psalm 21; Mark 1
22. Genesis 43-44; Psalm 22; Mark 2
23. Genesis 45-46; Psalm 23; Mark 3
24. Genesis 47-48; Psalm 24; Mark 4
25. Genesis 49-50; Psalm 25; Mark 5
26. Exodus 1-2; Psalm 26; Mark 6
27. Exodus 3-4; Psalm 27; Mark 7
28. Exodus 5-6; Psalm 28; Mark 8
29. Exodus 7-8; Psalm 29; Mark 9
30. Exodus 9-10; Psalm 30; Mark 10
31. Exodus 11-12; Psalm 31; Mark 11

FEBRUARY

1. Exodus 13-14; Psalm 32; Mark 12
2. Exodus 15-16; Psalm 33; Mark 13
3. Exodus 17-18; Psalm 34; Mark 14
4. Exodus 19-20; Psalm 35; Mark 15
5. Exodus 21-22; Psalm 36; Mark 16
6. Exodus 23-24; Psalm 37; Luke 1
7. Exodus 25-26; Psalm 38; Luke 2
8. Exodus 27-28; Psalm 39; Luke 3
9. Exodus 29-30; Psalm 40; Luke 4
10. Exodus 31-32; Psalm 41; Luke 5
11. Exodus 33-34; Psalm 42; Luke 6
12. Exodus 35-36; Psalm 43; Luke 7
13. Exodus 37-38; Psalm 44; Luke 8
14. Exodus 39-40; Psalm 45; Luke 9
15. Leviticus 1-2; Psalm 46; Luke 10
16. Leviticus 3-4; Psalm 47; Luke 11
17. Leviticus 5-6; Psalm 48; Luke 12
18. Leviticus 7-8; Psalm 49; Luke 13
19. Leviticus 9-10; Psalm 50; Luke 14
20. Leviticus 11-12; Psalm 51; Luke 15
21. Leviticus 13; Psalm 52; Luke 16
22. Leviticus 14; Psalm 53; Luke 17
23. Leviticus 15-16; Psalm 54; Luke 18
24. Leviticus 17-18; Psalm 55; Luke 19
25. Leviticus 19-20; Psalm 56; Luke 20
26. Leviticus 21-22; Psalm 57; Luke 21
27. Leviticus 23-24; Psalm 58; Luke 22
28. Leviticus 25; Psalm 59; Luke 23

MARCH

1. Leviticus 26-27; Psalm 60; Luke 24
2. Numbers 1-2; Psalm 61; John 1
3. Numbers 3-4; Psalm 62; John 2-3
4. Numbers 5-6; Psalm 63; John 4
5. Numbers 7; Psalm 64; John 5
6. Numbers 8-9; Psalm 65; John 6
7. Numbers 10-11; Psalm 66; John 7
8. Numbers 12-13; Psalm 67; John 8
9. Numbers 14-15; Psalm 68; John 9
10. Numbers 16; Psalm 69; John 10
11. Numbers 17-18; Psalm 70; John 11
12. Numbers 19-20; Psalm 71; John 12
13. Numbers 21-22; Psalm 72; John 13
14. Numbers 23-24; Psalm 73; John 14-15
15. Numbers 25-26; Psalm 74; John 16
16. Numbers 27-28; Psalm 75; John 17
17. Numbers 29-30; Psalm 76; John 18
18. Numbers 31-32; Psalm 77; John 19
19. Numbers 33-34; Psalm 78; John 20
20. Numbers 35-36; Psalm 79; John 21
21. Deuteronomy 1-2; Psalm 80; Acts 1
22. Deuteronomy 3-4; Psalm 81; Acts 2
23. Deuteronomy 5-6; Psalm 82; Acts 3-4
24. Deuteronomy 7-8; Psalm 83; Acts 5-6
25. Deuteronomy 9-10; Psalm 84; Acts 7
26. Deuteronomy 11-12; Psalm 85; Acts 8
27. Deuteronomy 13-14; Psalm 86; Acts 9
28. Deuteronomy 15-16; Psalm 87; Acts 10
29. Deuteronomy 17-18; Psalm 88; Acts 11-12
30. Deuteronomy 19-20; Psalm 89; Acts 13
31. Deuteronomy 21-22; Psalm 90; Acts 14

APRIL

1. Deuteronomy 23-24; Psalm 91; Acts 15
2. Deuteronomy 25-27; Psalm 92; Acts 16
3. Deuteronomy 28-29; Psalm 93; Acts 17
4. Deuteronomy 30-31; Psalm 94; Acts 18
5. Deuteronomy 32; Psalm 95; Acts 19
6. Deuteronomy 33-34; Psalm 96; Acts 20
7. Joshua 1-2; Psalm 97; Acts 21
8. Joshua 3-4; Psalm 98; Acts 22
9. Joshua 5-6; Psalm 99; Acts 23
10. Joshua 7-8; Psalm 100; Acts 24-25
11. Joshua 9-10; Psalm 101; Acts 26
12. Joshua 11-12; Psalm 102; Acts 27
13. Joshua 13-14; Psalm 103; Acts 28
14. Joshua 15-16; Psalm 104; Romans 1-2
15. Joshua 17-18; Psalm 105; Romans 3-4
16. Joshua 19-20; Psalm 106; Romans 5-6
17. Joshua 21-22; Psalm 107; Romans 7-8
18. Joshua 23-24; Psalm 108; Romans 9-10
19. Judges 1-2; Psalm 109; Romans 11-12
20. Judges 3-4; Psalm 110; Romans 13-14
21. Judges 5-6; Psalm 111; Romans 15-16
22. Judges 7-8; Psalm 112; 1 Corinthians 1-2
23. Judges 9; Psalm 113; 1 Corinthians 3-4
24. Judges 10-11; Psalm 114; 1 Corinthians 5-6
25. Judges 12-13; Psalm 115; 1 Corinthians 7
26. Judges 14-15; Psalm 116; 1 Corinthians 8-9
27. Judges 16-17; Psalm 117; 1 Corinthians 10
28. Judges 18-19; Psalm 118; 1 Corinthians 11
29. Judges 20-21; Psalm 119:1-88; 1 Corinthians 12
30. Ruth 1-4; Psalm 119:89-176; 1 Corinthians 13

MAY

1. 1 Samuel 1-2; Psalm 120; 1 Corinthians 14
2. 1 Samuel 3-4; Psalm 121; 1 Corinthians 15
3. 1 Samuel 5-6; Psalm 122; 1 Corinthians 16
4. 1 Samuel 7-8; Psalm 123; 2 Corinthians 1
5. 1 Samuel 9-10; Psalm 124; 2 Corinthians 2-3
6. 1 Samuel 11-12; Psalm 125; 2 Corinthians 4-5
7. 1 Samuel 13-14; Psalm 126; 2 Corinthians 6-7
8. 1 Samuel 15-16; Psalm 127; 2 Corinthians 8
9. 1 Samuel 17; Psalm 128; 2 Corinthians 9-10
10. 1 Samuel 18-19; Psalm 129; 2 Corinthians 11
11. 1 Samuel 20-21; Psalm 130; 2 Corinthians 12
12. 1 Samuel 22-23; Psalm 131; 2 Corinthians 13
13. 1 Samuel 24-25; Psalm 132; Galatians 1-2
14. 1 Samuel 26-27; Psalm 133; Galatians 3-4
15. 1 Samuel 28-29; Psalm 134; Galatians 5-6
16. 1 Samuel 30-31; Psalm 135; Ephesians 1-2
17. 2 Samuel 1-2; Psalm 136; Ephesians 3-4
18. 2 Samuel 3-4; Psalm 137; Ephesians 5-6
19. 2 Samuel 5-6; Psalm 138; Philippians 1-2
20. 2 Samuel 7-8; Psalm 139; Philippians 3-4
21. 2 Samuel 9-10; Psalm 140; Colossians 1-2
22. 2 Samuel 11-12; Psalm 141; Colossians 3-4
23. 2 Samuel 13-14; Psalm 142; 1 Thessalonians 1-2
24. 2 Samuel 15-16; Psalm 143; 1 Thessalonians 3-4
25. 2 Samuel 17-18; Psalm 144; 1 Thessalonians 5
26. 2 Samuel 19; Psalm 145; 2 Thessalonians 1-3
27. 2 Samuel 20-21; Psalm 146; 1 Timothy 1-2
28. 2 Samuel 22; Psalm 147; 1 Timothy 3-4
29. 2 Samuel 23-24; Psalm 148; 1 Timothy 5-6
30. 1 Kings 1; Psalm 149; 2 Timothy 1-2
31. 1 Kings 2-3; Psalm 150; 2 Timothy 3-4

JUNE

1. 1 Kings 4-5; Proverbs 1; Titus 1-3
2. 1 Kings 6-7; Proverbs 2; Philemon
3. 1 Kings 8; Proverbs 3; Hebrews 1-2
4. 1 Kings 9-10; Proverbs 4; Hebrews 3-4
5. 1 Kings 11-12; Proverbs 5; Hebrews 5-6
6. 1 Kings 13-14; Proverbs 6; Hebrews 7-8
7. 1 Kings 15-16; Proverbs 7; Hebrews 9-10
8. 1 Kings 17-18; Proverbs 8; Hebrews 11
9. 1 Kings 19-20; Proverbs 9; Hebrews 12
10. 1 Kings 21-22; Proverbs 10; Hebrews 13
11. 2 Kings 1-2; Proverbs 11; James 1
12. 2 Kings 3-4; Proverbs 12; James 2-3
13. 2 Kings 5-6; Proverbs 13; James 4-5
14. 2 Kings 7-8; Proverbs 14; 1 Peter 1
15. 2 Kings 9-10; Proverbs 15; 1 Peter 2-3
16. 2 Kings 11-12; Proverbs 16; 1 Peter 4-5
17. 2 Kings 13-14; Proverbs 17; 2 Peter 1-3
18. 2 Kings 15-16; Proverbs 18; 1 John 1-2
19. 2 Kings 17; Proverbs 19; 1 John 3-4
20. 2 Kings 18-19; Proverbs 20; 1 John 5
21. 2 Kings 20-21; Proverbs 21; 2 John
22. 2 Kings 22-23; Proverbs 22; 3 John
23. 2 Kings 24-25; Proverbs 23; Jude
24. 1 Chronicles 1; Proverbs 24; Revelation 1-2
25. 1 Chronicles 2-3; Proverbs 25; Revelation 3-5
26. 1 Chronicles 4-5; Proverbs 26; Revelation 6-7
27. 1 Chronicles 6-7; Proverbs 27; Revelation 8-10
28. 1 Chronicles 8-9; Proverbs 28; Revelation 11-12
29. 1 Chronicles 10-11; Proverbs 29; Revelation 13-14
30. 1 Chronicles 12-13; Proverbs 30; Revelation 15-17

JULY

1. 1 Chronicles 14-15; Proverbs 31; Revelation 18-19
2. 1 Chronicles 16-17; Psalm 1; Revelation 20-22
3. 1 Chronicles 18-19; Psalm 2; Matthew 1-2
4. 1 Chronicles 20-21; Psalm 3; Matthew 3-4
5. 1 Chronicles 22-23; Psalm 4; Matthew 5
6. 1 Chronicles 24-25; Psalm 5; Matthew 6-7
7. 1 Chronicles 26-27; Psalm 6; Matthew 8-9
8. 1 Chronicles 28-29; Psalm 7; Matthew 10-11
9. 2 Chronicles 1-2; Psalm 8; Matthew 12
10. 2 Chronicles 3-4; Psalm 9; Matthew 13
11. 2 Chronicles 5-6; Psalm 10; Matthew 14-15
12. 2 Chronicles 7-8; Psalm 11; Matthew 16-17
13. 2 Chronicles 9-10; Psalm 12; Matthew 18
14. 2 Chronicles 11-12; Psalm 13; Matthew 19-20
15. 2 Chronicles 13-14; Psalm 14; Matthew 21
16. 2 Chronicles 15-16; Psalm 15; Matthew 22
17. 2 Chronicles 17-18; Psalm 16; Matthew 23
18. 2 Chronicles 19-20; Psalm 17; Matthew 24
19. 2 Chronicles 21-22; Psalm 18; Matthew 25
20. 2 Chronicles 23-24; Psalm 19; Matthew 26
21. 2 Chronicles 25-26; Psalm 20; Matthew 27
22. 2 Chronicles 27-28; Psalm 21; Matthew 28
23. 2 Chronicles 29-30; Psalm 22; Mark 1
24. 2 Chronicles 31-32; Psalm 23; Mark 2
25. 2 Chronicles 33-34; Psalm 24; Mark 3
26. 2 Chronicles 35-36; Psalm 25; Mark 4
27. Ezra 1-2; Psalm 26; Mark 5
28. Ezra 3-4; Psalm 27; Mark 6
29. Ezra 5-6; Psalm 28; Mark 7
30. Ezra 7-8; Psalm 29; Mark 8
31. Ezra 9-10; Psalm 30; Mark 9

AUGUST

1. Nehemiah 1-2; Psalm 31; Mark 10
2. Nehemiah 3-4; Psalm 32; Mark 11
3. Nehemiah 5-6; Psalm 33; Mark 12
4. Nehemiah 7; Psalm 34; Mark 13
5. Nehemiah 8-9; Psalm 35; Mark 14
6. Nehemiah 10-11; Psalm 36; Mark 15
7. Nehemiah 12-13; Psalm 37; Mark 16
8. Esther 1-2; Psalm 38; Luke 1
9. Esther 3-4; Psalm 39; Luke 2
10. Esther 5-6; Psalm 40; Luke 3
11. Esther 7-8; Psalm 41; Luke 4
12. Esther 9-10; Psalm 42; Luke 5
13. Job 1-2; Psalm 43; Luke 6
14. Job 3-4; Psalm 44; Luke 7
15. Job 5-6; Psalm 45; Luke 8
16. Job 7-8; Psalm 46; Luke 9
17. Job 9-10; Psalm 47; Luke 10
18. Job 11-12; Psalm 48; Luke 11
19. Job 13-14; Psalm 49; Luke 12
20. Job 15-16; Psalm 50; Luke 13
21. Job 17-18; Psalm 51; Luke 14
22. Job 19-20; Psalm 52; Luke 15
23. Job 21-22; Psalm 53; Luke 16
24. Job 23-25; Psalm 54; Luke 17
25. Job 26-28; Psalm 55; Luke 18
26. Job 29-30; Psalm 56; Luke 19
27. Job 31-32; Psalm 57; Luke 20
28. Job 33-34; Psalm 58; Luke 21
29. Job 35-36; Psalm 59; Luke 22
30. Job 37-38; Psalm 60; Luke 23
31. Job 39-40; Psalm 61; Luke 24

SEPTEMBER

1. Job 41-42; Psalm 62; John 1
2. Ecclesiastes 1-2; Psalm 63; John 2-3
3. Ecclesiastes 3-4; Psalm 64; John 4
4. Ecclesiastes 5-6; Psalm 65; John 5
5. Ecclesiastes 7-8; Psalm 66; John 6
6. Ecclesiastes 9-10; Psalm 67; John 7
7. Ecclesiastes 11-12; Psalm 68; John 8
8. Song of Solomon 1-2; Psalm 69; John 9
9. Song of Solomon 3-4; Psalm 70; John 10
10. Song of Solomon 5-6; Psalm 71; John 11
11. Song of Solomon 7-8; Psalm 72; John 12
12. Isaiah 1-2; Psalm 73; John 13
13. Isaiah 3-5; Psalm 74; John 14-15
14. Isaiah 6-8; Psalm 75; John 16
15. Isaiah 9-10; Psalm 76; John 17
16. Isaiah 11-13; Psalm 77; John 18
17. Isaiah 14-15; Psalm 78; John 19
18. Isaiah 16-17; Psalm 79; John 20
19. Isaiah 18-19; Psalm 80; John 21
20. Isaiah 20-22; Psalm 81; Acts 1
21. Isaiah 23-24; Psalm 82; Acts 2
22. Isaiah 25-26; Psalm 83; Acts 3-4
23. Isaiah 27-28; Psalm 84; Acts 5-6
24. Isaiah 29-30; Psalm 85; Acts 7
25. Isaiah 31-32; Psalm 86; Acts 8
26. Isaiah 33-34; Psalm 87; Acts 9
27. Isaiah 35-36; Psalm 88; Acts 10
28. Isaiah 37-38; Psalm 89; Acts 11-12
29. Isaiah 39-40; Psalm 90; Acts 13
30. Isaiah 41-42; Psalm 91; Acts 14

OCTOBER

1. Isaiah 43-44; Psalm 92; Acts 15
2. Isaiah 45-46; Psalm 93; Acts 16
3. Isaiah 47-48; Psalm 94; Acts 17
4. Isaiah 49-50; Psalm 95; Acts 18
5. Isaiah 51-52; Psalm 96; Acts 19
6. Isaiah 53-54; Psalm 97; Acts 20
7. Isaiah 55-56; Psalm 98; Acts 21
8. Isaiah 57-58; Psalm 99; Acts 22
9. Isaiah 59-60; Psalm 100; Acts 23
10. Isaiah 61-62; Psalm 101; Acts 24-25
11. Isaiah 63-64; Psalm 102; Acts 26
12. Isaiah 65-66; Psalm 103; Acts 27
13. Jeremiah 1-2; Psalm 104; Acts 28
14. Jeremiah 3-4; Psalm 105; Romans 1-2
15. Jeremiah 5-6; Psalm 106; Romans 3-4
16. Jeremiah 7-8; Psalm 107; Romans 5-6
17. Jeremiah 9-10; Psalm 108; Romans 7-8
18. Jeremiah 11-12; Psalm 109; Romans 9-10
19. Jeremiah 13-14; Psalm 110; Romans 11-12
20. Jeremiah 15-16; Psalm 111; Romans 13-14
21. Jeremiah 17-18; Psalm 112; Romans 15-16
22. Jeremiah 19-20; Psalm 113; 1 Corinthians 1-2
23. Jeremiah 21-22; Psalm 114; 1 Corinthians 3-4
24. Jeremiah 23-24; Psalm 115; 1 Corinthians 5-6
25. Jeremiah 25-26; Psalm 116; 1 Corinthians 7
26. Jeremiah 27-28; Psalm 117; 1 Corinthians 8-9
27. Jeremiah 29-30; Psalm 118; 1 Corinthians 10
28. Jeremiah 31-32; Psalm 119: 1-64; 1 Corinthians 11
29. Jeremiah 33-34; Psalm 119:65-120; 1 Corinthians 12
30. Jeremiah 35-36; Psalm 119:121-176;1 Corinthians 13
31. Jeremiah 37-38; Psalm 120; 1 Corinthians 14

NOVEMBER

1. Jeremiah 39-40; Psalm 121; 1 Corinthians 15
2. Jeremiah 41-42; Psalm 122; 1 Corinthians 16
3. Jeremiah 43-44; Psalm 123; 2 Corinthians 1
4. Jeremiah 45-46; Psalm 124; 2 Corinthians 2-3
5. Jeremiah 47-48; Psalm 125; 2 Corinthians 4-5
6. Jeremiah 49-50; Psalm 126; 2 Corinthians 6-7
7. Jeremiah 51-52; Psalm 127; 2 Corinthians 8
8. Lamentations 1-2; Psalm 128; 2 Corinthians 9-10
9. Lamentations 3; Psalm 129; 2 Corinthians 11
10. Lamentations 4-5; Psalm 130; 2 Corinthians 12
11. Ezekiel 1-2; Psalm 131; 2 Corinthians 13
12. Ezekiel 3-4; Psalm 132; Galatians 1-2
13. Ezekiel 5-6; Psalm 133; Galatians 3-4
14. Ezekiel 7-8; Psalm 134; Galatians 5-6
15. Ezekiel 9-10; Psalm 135; Ephesians 1-2
16. Ezekiel 11-12; Psalm 136; Ephesians 3-4
17. Ezekiel 13-14; Psalm 137; Ephesians 5-6
18. Ezekiel 15-16; Psalm 138; Philippians 1-2
19. Ezekiel 17-18; Psalm 139; Philippians 3-4
20. Ezekiel 19-20; Psalm 140; Colossians 1-2
21. Ezekiel 21-22; Psalm 141; Colossians 3-4
22. Ezekiel 23-24; Psalm 142; 1 Thessalonians 1-2
23. Ezekiel 25-26; Psalm 143; 1 Thessalonians 3-4
24. Ezekiel 27-28; Psalm 144; 1 Thessalonians 5
25. Ezekiel 29-30; Psalm 145; 2 Thessalonians 1-3
26. Ezekiel 31-32; Psalm 146; 1 Timothy 1-2
27. Ezekiel 33-34; Psalm 147; 1 Timothy 3-4
28. Ezekiel 35-36; Psalm 148; 1 Timothy 5-6
29. Ezekiel 37-38; Psalm 149; 2 Timothy 1-2
30. Ezekiel 39-40; Psalm 150; 2 Timothy 3-4

DECEMBER

1.   Ezekiel 41-42; Proverbs 1; Titus 1-3
2.   Ezekiel 43-44; Proverbs 2; Philemon
3.   Ezekiel 45-46; Proverbs 3; Hebrews 1-2
4.   Ezekiel 47-48; Proverbs 4; Hebrews 3-4
5.   Daniel 1-2; Proverbs 5; Hebrews 5-6
6.   Daniel 3-4; Proverbs 6; Hebrews 7-8
7.   Daniel 5-6; Proverbs 7; Hebrews 9-10
8.   Daniel 7-8; Proverbs 8; Hebrews 11
9.   Daniel 9-10; Proverbs 9; Hebrews 12
10. Daniel 11-12; Proverbs 10; Hebrews 13
11. Hosea 1-3; Proverbs 11; James 1-3
12. Hosea 4-6; Proverbs 12; James 4-5
13. Hosea 7-8; Proverbs 13; 1 Peter 1
14. Hosea 9-11; Proverbs 14; 1 Peter 2-3
15. Hosea 12-14; Proverbs 15; 1 Peter 4-5
16. Joel 1-3; Proverbs 16; 2 Peter 1-3
17. Amos 1-3; Proverbs 17; 1 John 1-2
18. Amos 4-6; Proverbs 18; 1 John 3-4
19. Amos 7-9; Proverbs 19; 1 John 5
20. Obadiah; Proverbs 20; 2 John
21. Jonah 1-4; Proverbs 21; 3 John
22. Micah 1-4; Proverbs 22; Jude
23. Micah 5-7; Proverbs 23; Revelation 1-2
24. Nahum 1-3; Proverbs 24; Revelation 3-5
25. Habakkuk 1-3; Proverbs 25; Revelation 6-7
26. Zephaniah 1-3; Proverbs 26; Revelation 8-10
27. Haggai 1-2; Proverbs 27; Revelation 11-12
28. Zechariah 1-4; Proverbs 28; Revelation 13-14
29. Zechariah 5-9; Proverbs 29; Revelation 15-17
30. Zechariah 10-14; Proverbs 30; Revelation 18-19
31. Malachi 1-4; Proverbs 31; Revelation 20-22

Acknowledgements

Harold Whitman (17), Author Unknown (19, 87, 89, 105, 123, 125, 139), Billy Graham (21), Thomas Aquinas (23, 95), Isaac Bashevis Singer (25), Pope John Paul II (27), John Maxwell (29), Mary Gardiner Brainard (31), Lyndon Baines Johnson (33), John Wanamaker (35), Francois Rabelais (39), John Henry Jowett, (41), Emily Elizabeth Dickinson (43), George MacDonald (45), Edwin Markham (47), Ralph Waldo Emerson (49, 143, 145), John Milton (51, 149), English Proverb (53), James Russell Lowell (55), Count Nikolaus Ludwig von Zinzendorf (57), Benjamin Harrison (59), Evelyn Underhill (61), Robert Robinson (63), Chinese Proverb (65, 155), Joachim Neander (67), Isaac Watts (69), E. B. Meyer (71, 81), Henry Ward Beecher (73), Henry Wadsworth Longfellow (75), Catherine of Siena (77), Henry Nouwen (79), James Montgomery (83), Francois F'enelon (85), Richard Holloway (91), Pascal (93), Reinhold Niebuhr (97), Tiruvalluvar (101), Alice Caldwell Rice (103), Hannah Whitall Smith (107), Therese of Lisieux (109), Emily Bronte (111, 169), Penelope Leach (113), François, Duc De La Rochefoucauld (115), Anne Frank (117), George Eliot (119), Mother Teresa of Calcutta (121, 133, 159), William Ralph Inge (127), Larry Lea (131), Mason Cooley (135), Mary Wallstonecraft (137), James L. Hymes Jr. (141), Jesus (147), Darienne Hall (151), Leonardo da Vinci (153), Marcus Tullius Cicero (157), Tomas a Kempis (161), Frederick William Faber (163), Jimmy Cater (165), Michael Ramsey, Archbishop of Canterbury (167), Faye T. Bresler (171), Abraham Lincoln (173), Henry David Thoreau (175), Gerard Manley Hopkins (177).

Additional copies of this and other
Honor Books products are available
wherever good books are sold.

A Pocketful of Promises for Women

If you have enjoyed this book,
or if it has had an impact on your life,
we would like to hear from you.

Please contact us at:

HONOR BOOKS
Cook Communications Ministries, Dept. 201
4050 Lee Vance View
Colorado Springs, CO 80918
Or visit our Web site:
www.cookministries.com

Inspiration and Motivation for the Season of Life